GOLD CARP JACK FRUIT MIRRORS

George Kalamaras

BITTER OLEANDER
P R E S S

The Bitter Oleander Press
Fayetteville, New York
2008

The Bitter Oleander Press
4983 Tall Oaks Drive
Fayetteville, New York 13066-9776
USA

www.bitteroleander.com
info@bitteroleander.com

First Edition

ISBN# 0-9786335-1-2

Library of Congress Control Number: 2007943530

Graphic Design & Layout:
Roderick Martinez Visual Communications
Liverpool, New York

Author Photograph: Jim Whitcraft

Cover Art: Alvaro Cardona-Hine "The Boddhisattvas," 1994

Printed by McNaughton & Gunn, Inc.
Saline, MI

Manufactured in the United States of America

GOLD
CARP
JACK
FRUIT
MIRRORS

Other Books by George Kalamaras

Poetry and Prose Poetry

Even the Java Sparrows Call Your Hair (2004)
Borders My Bent Toward (2003)
The Theory and Function of Mangoes (2000)

Poetry Chapbooks

Beneath the Breath (1988)
Heart Without End (1986)

Criticism

Reclaiming the Tacit Dimension: Symbolic Form in the Rhetoric of Silence (1994)

ACKNOWLEDGMENTS

The author thanks the editors of the following magazines in which some of these poems, or their previous versions, first appeared:

Antigonish Review (Canada): "The Atomic Weight of Dusk"

Arabesques (Algeria): "Getting the Tonguing Tender Enough"

The Bitter Oleander: "Banaras is Another Name for the World," "Dhobi Wallah" (1998 Frances Locke Poetry Award Finalist), "Convergence," "Landscape of the Dead," "Meeting Alison at the Malaviya Bhavan, Banaras Hindu University," and "At Red Fort"

Conjunctions Web: "Gold Carp Jack Fruit Mirrors"

The Drunken Boat: "Cut of the World" and "At the Ashram of Trailanga Swami"

First Intensity: "The Underwater Underside"

Florida Review: "Every Day at Three"

Folio: "Scales of Mother Ganga" and "A Theory of the Shape of Palms"

Louisiana Review: "A Theory of the Choke of Dust" and "Icon"

Luna: "Sacrifice"

Manhattan Review: "You Keep Coming Upon Your Breath at the Altar" and "Next Year When I Fish Hydrates in Fiscal Blue"

Many Mountains Moving: "In Bhelupur"

Marlboro Review: "As You Breathe in the Slouching"

Massachusetts Review: "Handling Fruit at a Calcutta Market"

Oyster Boy Review: "A Temple Pool Might Ignite (Lotus-Blood from Your Heart)"

Pavement Saw: "Karmic Seeds"

Quarterly West: "Jasmine"

Spoon River Poetry Review: "The Milk of Shadows" and "The Lamps Are Brought In"

Stand (United Kingdom): "A Theory of the Origin of Birth"

Terra Incognita: "The Crawl of Ash" and "Drinking Tea at a Silk Shop During Monson with Sons of an Independence Fighter"

The author also thanks the following for reprinting some of the preceding poems in their pages:

American Diaspora: Poetry of Exile (University of Iowa Press): "Jasmine"

The Drunken Boat: "Meeting Alison at the Malaviya Bhavan, Banaras Hindu University"

Pomegranate Seeds: An Anthology of Greek-American Poetry (Somerset Hall Press): "Banaras is Another Name for the World"

Vespers: Religion & Spirituality in Twenty-first Century America (Syracuse University Press)*:* "Banaras is Another Name for the World," "You Keep Coming Upon Your Breath at the Altar," and "The Lamps Are Brought In"

AUTHOR'S NOTE

I am grateful to the Fulbright Foreign Scholarship Board, the Indo-U.S. Subcommission on Education and Culture, and the American Institute of Indian Studies, whose generous assistance of an Indo-U.S. Advanced Research Fellowship made my months in India possible, as did a supplementary grant from the Office of International Programs, Indiana University.

Gratitude, as well, to the Indiana Arts Commission for an Individual Artist's Grant that supported this project, and to the Hambidge Center for the Arts, Rabun Gap, Georgia, for two writing residencies where I worked on this book.

Special thanks to my parents and all of my family, teachers, and friends (for love, encouragement, and insight) and to the following for their specific contributions:

Paul B. Roth (for unfailing support of my poetry and for taking this project on); Juan Felipe Herrera (for helping me see the title of the title poem within my own tangle of words); Alvaro Cardona-Hine and Marie Ponsot (poetic forebears, whose painting and words on the front and back cover, respectively, hold the pages of this book in a tender embrace); Forrest Gander, Noah Eli Gordon, Andrew Joron, John Olson, and Joshua Marie Wilkinson (for years of listening in on my work, even before I knew they were); Michael Patterson and John and Lisa Zimmerman (for poetic and spiritual companionship); Clark, Kim, and Ruth Waterfall (for lending me their Big Timber, Montana lodgings for three months to work on this book); Sue Tungate and the late Gene Hoffman (for letting me roost, read, and write in their northern Colorado home in Livermore on multiple occasions, for weeks on end—with plenty of silence and invaluable companionship); Bill and Cynthia Tremblay (for their continuing friendship and insights, and for wonderful conversation over coffee at the Western Ridge in Livermore); Anuradha Banerjee, Ranjit Hoskote, Awadhesh K. Mishra, Aruna Mukhopadhyay, and R. Raj Rao (for their many kindnesses during my stay in India); Eric Baus, John Bradley, Ray Gonzalez, Jim Grabill, Patrick Lawler, and Phil Woods (for being such important eyes, ears, and inspiration for my work for more years than I can count, and in more ways than I could ever describe); John Bradley (for his abundant insights into this book and his characteristic generosity in carefully reading and responding to nearly all of my poems); Mary Ann Cain (for being "the one" in all things we so sweetly share—meditation, writing, and love); and Paramahansa Yogananda (for first showing me the path of Yoga and nurturing the seeds of this journey—my "return" to India).

For Mary Ann
for this journey we share, again and again

and for the beloved yogis of modern and ancient India

and for Gene Frumkin and Mary Rising Higgins—
two remarkable poets, and their great breathing, now, among the trees

CONTENTS

GETTING THE TONGUING TENDER ENOUGH

THE SHAPE OF DISSOLVE

*Within the city of Brahman, which is the body, there is
the heart, and within the heart there is a little house. This
house has the shape of a lotus, and within it dwells that which
is to be sought after, inquired about, and realized.*

—*Chandogya Upanishad*
(tr. Swami Prabhavananda
and Frederick Manchester)

We did not dream enough in that house.

—Gaston Bachelard, *The Poetics of Space*
(tr. Maria Jolas)

AMONG GLOWING SCARS

THE CRAWL OF ASH

In the Banaras garden of your Bengali friends,
the world is fashioned from coconut shreds
and death. Life here is simple
and life takes its tone
from the sound of ash crawling
your name just a few lanes east
from the cremation grounds. At the river Ganges,
heavy iron combs keep the tongue
of a pilgrim in place. Two aniseeds
blow dark among glowing scars
of a man who, at dawn, approaches you
with a carp he's pulled from river muck.
A floating gold leaf is dulled by the scrawl
of small stones. Somewhere in your heart
its recent branch fastens the wind
around which charred remains of others
cull your molecular weight. Or
centuries of dark slags
into moist human skin. There *is* such a thing
as fear of loss, as your insides
shredding apart before the mirror
each morning from incarnation
to incarnation? As Bengali rice
placed before you on the plate, reflecting strains
of yourself you cannot refuse?
This, thirteen years in the past,
and every moment since is crushed Indiana
corn. This garden sprawling backward
toward river stone through threads
of raisins, cashews, and cruel coconut
milk. This ash, toward a fire of what
you might burn to become, or turn
away from time after time with what seems
a first and always brilliant birth.

BANARAS IS ANOTHER NAME FOR THE WORLD

JASMINE

There is no beginning and no end
to it, at least to the jasmine blossoms
she leans into in the court and shows
you. You want her to teach you
that highly developed sense of female
smell, how she can detect a gas leak
even amidst curry at home, or know
the dog's been rolling in dead birds, or sense
the coming of roses, but you don't know how
to ask. You shuffle out of your hotel
instead, hail a rickshaw and turn
to her, *Yeah, nice jasmines*, knowing you missed
some scent that might make you
whole and could save the world
if sniffed just right. Your entire life
you've struggled with it, how to say *no*
when you mean *no*, how to read the news
and stop the flood, how to stare at the phone
with perfect calm and not answer
and not run from room to room. You're six again
and crying when it rings, only this time inside
where the acid from your coffee stirs
My Friend Flicka and she kicks up
dust and the '62 Chevy is always
brand new. That eternal hope
of Lassie, say, or Rin Tin Tin, and new-car
smell in the way they lick a hand
and with a whimper make the healing
begin. You step onto the silver lip
of the rickshaw, feeling your weight,
sensing the odor of decades of sweat
on the cart seat, in the torn burlap
canopy that tousles your hair and makes you
feel like a kid at a wedding, smells

of possibility and pain in the musky cake
cutting and wine and slow-touching hips
of the last song, in the perfume
that lingers on the garter
and scent of silk that high, odors you don't yet know
the language of, like Hindi scrawled
in rain-soaked leather of the wallah's bicycle
seat, but older, like Sanskrit
script and lost. Where can you look,
you wonder, to decode the directions
for smell, even if it is red vinyl, ripped
and sun-bleached like old blood? Even
if it is the oil of so many unknown heads
rubbing up against yours through the sag
of the canopy, like dogs trying to find their way
among one another on the street? So you step onto
the lip and crush the seat and examine the sweat
that drips from the rickshaw wallah's lungi
wrapped around thighs, tucked between legs,
from the cracked rubber and salt-spill
of his thongs, from the peddling uphill
that always makes *your* shoulders ache afterwards
at night when you look in the mirror.
You want to smell it all, to know
when the bird has fallen, to anticipate
the roses, to bury the stallions
and pick up the receiver for once
without the dust and kicking
in your gut. To turn toward your wife
and graze her palm where the scent
remains in cracks like star charts
we are given to learn
the birth of blossoms
and thorns, the new and the torn.
To smell jasmine in an uphill

climb and enormous dignity
in the difficult smile
given—even sweetness in the reaching for a rupee
and in the sudden turning and peddling away,
in burnt curry and crust in bottoms
of street-corner cauldrons or the wok
back home, and in the gas leak
that occasionally comes to remind you
who and what you are.

SACRIFICE

From the roof of your flat, you see Ganga
for the first time and realize why cobras

are venerated throughout India.
Sitar shade takes a corner of the roof,

and you step away from the sun to see
more clearly its burn in the scales of a snake.

As a child, you drank skim milk and wondered
if there were skinny cows who gave it.

Now you see snows of the Himalayas
thin out but widen as they wind through the lower plains.

This is where Brahma sacrificed hundreds of horses.
You feel their blood as you turn to see

miles and miles of flood to the south.
To be marched down to the river, oiled,

perfumed, and sang to. To have your throat slit
and the bulk of your years dropped with a splash,

a massive bag of feed that jerks like
a huge hooked bass. To have your blood thin out

into lines of laundry, river stone, brass
bowls, cooking fires, soup, soap, table salt,

is to die to yourself but prance in the plants,
snort in scales of a glittering

snake, in the dash of a goat as it splashes the flood
of the river it drinks, back into the pail.

THE MILK OF SHADOWS

A Brahmin woman leaving Durga Temple
in Banaras steps into the shadow

of an untouchable. For three days
she does not speak to her son and is finally cleansed

by a priest's candle and rattle of maracas
in her right ear. In the temple and monastery

caves of Ajanta, a caterpillar is trailed, mistaken
for a leech, stepped on, and decapitated

beneath a torch-lit fresco of Buddha
by a man shouting, *Gandhiji was an idealist!*

A Mewar revivalist folk artist who paints miniatures
of copulating Moguls in Maharashtra dreams one night

that the Hindu Nationalist Party has confiscated
his brushes, then wakes to find that he wants

only to paint by starlight burning giraffes
and lava flows of goldfish. You hold

a glost of tea, drink chai brown with water-buffalo
milk, have flown a long way with the sun at your back

to get here: South Bend, Cincinnati, New York,
Frankfurt, Delhi, Banaras. You have crossed

the dateline mostly without shade over ocean
sometime during shallow sleep

to arrive in smoky Banaras with only the dance
of cooking fires to guide you and a pale broth

of moon. You follow narrow cobblestone
lanes, sipping chai, stunned by the absence of light—

here on the other side of the earth—
and the sudden folds of dark turbans

at the edge of town huddled over cauldrons
hiding Mercury and Mars somewhere

in black beans. A sadhu from Basohli
steps out of the shadows, rubs earth

on his penis, ties a sling of cloth
around it, stretches his legs, and lifts with it

four blocks of roadstone to demonstrate
his transcendence of sexuality, his growth

toward the light of God. His penis lengthens
like the nipple of a tugged udder,

or jack fruit slung too long on a tree.
Moonlight pours milk into your cup,

thickening chai. Glistening drops of sperm
on the murky hairs of his pubis.

BANARAS IS ANOTHER NAME FOR THE WORLD

A sadhu carries a lamp to the Ganges,
unwinds his long hair into the river.

The Milky Way glitters in mud, twigs,
snags of carp, and ashes of millions.

Were they content over the evening dal?
Did they like tea? How were they touched?

Banaras is another name for the world.
Ganga, for the mother of the world.

You count goats on the steps of the bathing ghat
and consider a new profession.

Maybe the chai wallah understands
the goats better than the goatherd?

New constellations form in the pail. Sagittarius
is not a mineral deficiency detailed in stools.

Whenever opposites attract, cobblestones shift a little and
the street curves inward at an almost undetectable slope.

You wander old Muslim neighborhoods on Madanpura
on your way to Chowk, sense the love of God even in cooking meat.

See how smoke from cremation grounds speckles the river?
You want to step in but you've seen the dead cow.

You've seen the purple corpse when you took the boat.
You've seen the men urinating against the wall.

Where is the gold carp and where is your foot?
How might you bathe in the river without getting in?

IN BHELUPUR

A child in Bhelupur is eating tangerine rinds
and cow dung in a pool of motor oil.

The waiter in Aces Restaurant puts his hand down his pants
and scratches his balls, as he stands at the table

to chat with the new American customers
who came for the advertised "health food."

Has the air conditioner back in your flat on Lanka burned
up yet? Has it frozen the fruit pits of your prayer beads

and your books on meditative calm? Has it fused the fringe
of your prayer rug with the sparkler sound of another power

surge? Men carry another corpse to the Ganges,
burn it, rake its ash through river-bottom mud.

It's all in a day's work.
Where is the gold tooth when you need it?

Where is the gold tooth you never got?
And why did you refuse a napkin at lunch

as a coaster for your bottle of Limca?
Now *your* scrotum begins to itch. You suddenly crave

Indian sweatmeats, a hot cup of chai, bits
of cardamom seed, maybe even an evening of Mogul love.

Ten or twelve wives say your name moistly with secret hair
across your pillow. Where does the freon

from Bhelupur in Banaras go when it is emitted?
The moon casts a cool halo even in 115-degree night?

A naked sadhu covered in cremation ash and garlands
of bees sits in full lotus in an alley of rotting produce,

chants one of the many names of God, has an aura
of goldenrod that grabs you where it hurts.

HANDLING FRUIT AT A CALCUTTA MARKET

You might have been here before,
but if you had you'd remember. Cabbage leaves
strewn in the alley, fruit flies caul-like
around a mango. A Calcutta cow no one seems to see.

Then the monsoon rains come, dust swirls
tiny funnel clouds, and you hear
a voice, *You have left home. If you stay here,*
thousands of miles away, you will be home.

The sand absorbs it, the gravel gives in,
the plaid of your shirt begins to drift
into something less solid. Yesterday, the one-armed man
near the Ganges held out to you something you remembered

burying in sixth-grade math, plunged into the darkness
of a chessboard or Parcheesi cup. The King ignored it.
The Queen held it in her skirts. The Bishops were blind.
The elephants, black or white and dumb.

It's time to square things off. It's time to exhume
the dice and discover entrails of bees. It's time to hear
a humming galaxy inside a cowry shell, in the soft
skin that has stiffened over the crown of your head

like horse blankets cured in blood. You step into a stall,
see mangoes overripe and punctured with worms,
are startled by the crush of a baby's cry
and the accent of a mother's palm pressing your arm

with *Baba please*, then pointing to her mouth
in exaggerated tenderness. Wreathes of bees
follow a wandering sadhu who carries a brass pot
to the river. Something has stung your left little finger

as you handle the pears. You see a small white dot,
like a miniature fist, tug a moment of blood.
Everything is moving fast. You glimpse a rat
the size of a cat for the first time in your life.

WHAT IS OPEN

You leave Chowringhee for Calcutta's south
sector, pass evening cooking fires that swell

sores of lepers that ooze red flecks in smog.
You leave Chowringhee, search for the yogi's

home, a Bengali harmonium,
to help you hear the name of God in dirt

or slanted light through palm fronds thick with diesel
dust. *Avoid Calcutta's unhealthy monsoon*

from June until the end of September,
your guidebook warns. You depend on splinters

of kerosene to light a difference. To help you
sidestep open sewers hidden within

flooded streets. To steady your gaze
to that of a cobra. To guide your rickshaw

wallah through narrow lanes
without names, avoiding the drag in his stance

and direct eye contact and how much
older he looks than you at forty. To help you

feel at a stall the ripeness of jack fruit
not as cholera and one of 8,000

annual city deaths during the rains,
but as a way home through smoldering

kettles and kerosene stoves and years of diesel
fumes dressing street corners with soot—something

solid, like a closed manhole,
or a rickshaw wheel in Calcutta rotating

slowly through street flood without braiding your name
to this place. Or corn thousands of miles

away, waist-high in August. In Fort Wayne,
Indiana, not far from Zesto Ice Cream,

honey and cream kernels within silk must be
swaying, *Taste me, brother, and die to yourself.*

You melt at this moment of mixed blood,
the incision point of sun in rain.

You leave Chowringhee. You leave the water
filter pumped at the source of the guest lodge

of the American Institute
of Indian Studies. You leave a heart-

beat in an unexpected hair
in a spoonful of curry. You leave the valve

that connects you to an entire season
of piss and shit, that converts the semen

and the table salt, the moon in the sag
of the sweeper woman's left breast and the water-buffalo

milk that thins your corn flakes each morning to slush.
You leave the hose and valve that take the slosh

of human giving, giving way to good
grace, clean intestines, unclogged sinuses,

and a snakeskin heart. All the pores of the leper
are yours if your breath would but scrawl

your name across her gauze black as scabs in your own
right ear. The canker sore on your tongue

is memory enough of what is open for you
in this city, and what is closed.

YOU KEEP COMING UPON YOUR BREATH
AT THE ALTAR

Has he walked away from the temple? Has he taken your shoes?
Your socks with those red sandstone stains?

Durga Temple had been hot yesterday, the floor wet
from the hose. Thousands of prayers clung to you as you walked.

Today at the Ananda Moyi Ma Temple, you try to lose
your breath to the cooling swell of incense.

How many died during the Indian Mutiny, you're not sure.
Were British bullets really greased with pig fat? With the fat of a cow?

And how might one know if a touch is real,
or just flesh? Moist, or simply tongue?

You keep coming upon your breath at the altar, imagine
walking home barefoot through alleys of broken glass.

A rumor may kill. A remote goat bell on the steps
of the ghat somehow sounds thunder off the river.

Cremation ash drifts by like wedges of night,
tiny bats dropping into the Ganges current.

Takahashi Shinkichi said, *The sparrow is the mightiest creature
in the world*, but you're certain he was never in Banaras in May.

You keep coming back to breath, restlessly stirring
thoughts, coming upon an altar and a sleeping snake.

If the breath would calm, the snake might lift its great golden head
for you to polish. Might open its mouth, unwind its tail.

The mosquito net over your bed somehow comes untucked
in the middle of each night. Death becomes almost holy.

It is talked about in the streets, whispered on corners
as eel-fire, given as diksha in the ashram, as sex on the cot.

Even eaten as over-spiced dal. It is rubbed with rags,
with cigarette butts. With turmeric and broiled beets.

In Bombay, your friends could not control the rubbing,
told you, *Getting malaria would one day be our fate.*

See: the paper tallies floods and tells you how to die.
The astrologer finds milk, even in the testicles of Taurus.

Now the temple priest brings prasad, sanctified sweets.
Hundreds of ants as thin brown veins in the little balls.

You keep coming upon tiny electrical currents
zigzagging lightning on the altar of the spine.

You keep coming upon breath, the flit of a sparrow
bringing you bone bruise as song.

You open your eyes, see the mat outside, the old man,
your shoes, a singeing bat. Even food at your feet.

Baksheesh for the old man guarding my shoes, you think.
Two rupees should be enough to tell you you're still alive.

THE LAMPS ARE BROUGHT IN

Mother Kali, the destroyer, is the giver
of all life. Then the doors in the spine open

and the lamps are brought in. The allergist
gives himself an injection of eelgrass

and tree pollen, foams at the mouth, wonders
if the bumps on his skin are real

or imagined. The motorcycle parked
by the peepal tree draws more flies

than the water buffalo on campus bathing in monsoon
mud. Can you feel heat lightning in your palm

as you enter the library and gnaw on a rubber hose?
Slap it across the back of a braying

donkey who chews prayer beads in the back
of a Tantric text? As you touch the uncurved

leather, longing for it to be round and bruised
with spokes? As you paint the walls of your puja room

with the ocher robes of a Hindu holy man and have visions
of an ancient fertility cult passing a goldfish

around a fire, chanting your name
centuries before your birth? Can you hear

molecules of struggle in a tuba tossed in a rut
to rust in the pen of some Banaras pig farm?

You can trade malaria pills on the black market
for vegetable pakora, careful

to have the skins boiled and peeled?
Under Kali's feet, Lord Shiva's prostrate body,

though appearing dead, is not dead.
His erect penis beneath the curve

of her full blue thighs is the giver
of all life. Then the doors in the spine open

and you hear the bleeding of crickets
in your groin. Threads of running water. A faucet

that drops filaments of the Milky Way
down through your medulla

into your scrotum. A piece of rope burns
like a piranha in southern summer shoals.

Gold carp, gold carp, gold carp, the rishi
chants in Sanskrit, drawing your outline in the mud.

The hanged man is a peyote blossom on the tip
of a cactus. No, the hanged man has an erection,

then an ejaculation at the precise moment
of death. He sways from a peepal tree

on India's northern plain like a bloated prayer flag
or a massive bag of feed before all who pass.

A moment of table salt you might think
twice about before seasoning the lamb.

THE UNDERWATER UNDERSIDE

DHOBI WALLAH

He comes each morning and asks for clothes,
how what you wear might give him pants,
potatoes, cardamom seed, and maybe a bit of betel nut
and a moist pan leaf for lonely Saturday nights.
Laundry washing, sir? Laundry washing? he repeats
at seven with an earthquake knock on your hotel door,
as if the pounding might make it happen,
as if the pounding might show you the strength
of the Ganges River rock he'll beat
your clothes against, and the passion of his
slapping, as if the pounding
might make it right. Finally, you figure centuries
kept you apart. Oceans thrust you onto different
shores—a bit of wayward sperm here, a blood-bathed
egg there—beating back your attempt
at tongues, at lanterns,
and sitting together for bread. You figure
some hole in the earth, some mound
of dirt, threw you together in fear or
hope, kept you looking over your shoulder at banana
leaves or Indiana corn, at browner skin
or bleach, at shinier or coarser hair, a fierce
waggling of heads like millions of tiny bees
on a rhododendron. Finally, the feeding is enough
to open a sore in your own belly and feel
the weight of space. You gather
your clothes like a loose, white bouquet—
underwear mostly, a week of socks and shorts,
and that one kurta and pajama you got
from the Gandhi Ashram on Lanka. You gather the secret
foot skin, the stench of temple floors rolled
and banded into fraying threads, the urine stains
and dark spots only you handle at home,
delicately, like bruises you might find
along the inner thigh, like a canker sore

you tongue in secret sometimes when talking
at work, or handling pears
in the market, or while having a flat tire
fixed, fascinated with the hole,
though the tonguing always makes it hurt worse.
Finally, the feeding is enough
for him to find light in his step as his body begins
to betray how badly he needs the job
and how fast he'll work if you give him the chance.
You gather what no one sees, what even you
rarely really see, what stays with you
daily, year upon year, closing your toes, cupping
your penis, your scrotum, like a delicate and kind
hand, circling with firmness the river moon
of your waist. And the offerings. You gather
the offerings, what your body emits to this embrace,
musk among yaks. You hand him
what no one sees and catch his index finger
enter by chance a stained and open flap. A fly
circles this pile, and the buzzing is enough
to fill the silence your Hindi and his English
work. This perfect stranger,
who will perfectly handle the tucks and tongues
against river rock and let the Ganges in.

CONVERGENCE

In Calcutta monsoon, a man argues with his wife
over the cost of okra, slams the door,

and walks to work in a foot of water. He plunges
into and drowns in a hidden manhole uncovered

to clear the streets of rain. That night,
his wife feeds vegetable korma

in silence to her kids, and the entire family
begins weeping all at once when the youngest spits

out his okra and demands, *More water!*
Is a moment of love or pain limited only to you,

or does it grow in those you breathe or touch,
pressed against their chests like an enlarged heart?

An old woman in Mysore gives her ailing aunt
pods of tamarind, cured in salt and mixed

with molasses and water, as a sherbet
against heat stroke, rocks her head

in her lap, singing in broken British,
You are my sunshine, my only sunshine.

You recall your mother threatening you
over beets with the emaciated image of children

in India. Poaching tigers in Bihar
may protect a village and its livestock,

but can the crushed bones really cure rheumatism,
convulsions, scabies, boils, dysentery, ulcers,

typhoid, malaria, even prolapse of the anus?
Can ground tiger bone scattered on the roof

actually end nightmares, or does one simply dream
in Calcutta of neighing horses that float

across pastures in Georgia, while the dozing grocer
across town dreams he walks on water to farm lotuses

and then suddenly gets stabbed in the ribs
by the horn of a Brahma bull in his kitchen

when he can't make chutney fast enough to please
the national cricket team unexplainably camped there?

Can an elixir of mushed tiger testicles
sold in Vietnam really grant "six lovemakings a night

to give birth to four sons"? And if so,
why can't two more suddenly wake

in wombs in Norway and Argentina? All this
gets complicated by your urge to die

to *left* and *right*, *this* and *that*. You consider
the differing inflections you use in Hindi for *yes*

and *no*, wonder how those sounds affect the inner
rhythms for God of those you meet

on the street. Moonlight on the Taj Mahal
may not mean that a widow in Uruguay is pregnant

at menopause but may touch you
proleptically, as you drink blended fruit

and yogurt the following morning in Agra
and abruptly answer another vendor, *Nahin*,

Nahin, without knowing from where
he approaches you, why, and with what.

THE UNDERWATER UNDERSIDE

They say peacock saliva enters the arteries
and feathers the heart at the precise moment

of silk. They say the body tightens one fierce instant
in its milky desire to be loose. They say holy men

in huts wear brown prayer beads to attract camel hair
and sodium in their water. They say *yes* means *no*, or

maybe, or *sometime-after-eight*. They say *Baba, please*,
and experience a rush like bars of chocolate melting

down or sugar bouillon dissolving in their veins.
I am an underwater underside, you hear in the street,

certain you've mistaken the scrape of a bicycle tire
for salt. You look out across makeshift fruit stalls

on Lanka and see a jungle of propped playing cards,
wonder what each vendor is really holding

when he offers you jack fruit. A pear
tossed near the curb, a discarded radio battery,

a cracked red bangle draped around a burning cigarette
butt—could mean that while you slept

they secretly replaced your liver
with an extra kidney. You sprinkle the jasmine

outside your hotel with a bit of boiled water,
consider the many ways dysentery finds

to enter one's spine. The electrons malaria spills
to avoid Maloprim and become the shaking

in the clock. Paths egrets take
when you suddenly wake to the migratory finch

of sparrows squaring in your skull.
Less is really more, you wonder? What goes around

comes from a cassava root in Sri Lanka
near the supposed graves of Cain and Abel?

A dehydration headache in Banaras is your turning
away from another three years from now

when she will unexpectedly irritate
the hell out of you one evening in a Florida kitchen,

with unresolved hair from high school, and then try
to apologize with a kiss. All radio waves continue

to cultivate asparagus, increase tribes
of chest hair, locate a new breed of shoes

in pond spills of lily pads.
You wonder what's playing tonight

at the Lalita Cinema. Why your English
to Greek dictionary can't decipher Hindi

show tunes. What contributes to the long queue
and starched shirts. What a song of unrequited love,

bleached, perfectly lined teeth, and exposed shoulders
on the set say about turbaned scotch

and dark cab rides and girls on smelly cots
on the Malabar Coast. You've been away a long time

and not long at all. The odor on your
feet might be cow urine or orange flower water,

but you can't tell because you're certain
they've replaced your kidney with the ticking

of a clock. Your spleen with a braid
of black, shiny hair. The light in your cells

with sodium-free camel water. Jasmine blossoms
outside your window are egrets boiling

in the chlorinated chill. Drinking thick, milky tea
moves you to rub spit in slow circles

on your left shoulder beneath blankets, makes you
want to kiss exposed brown bellies in moonlight?

You need to know why, even with your hotel door
open, you feel so all alone.

LANDSCAPE OF THE DEAD

In monsoon afternoon, a sari dealer
hands you a teacup. Empty, you wonder

just what you're doing in Banaras.
In Frankfurt, they smoked throughout the airport.

Vultures circled Delhi sky above Lodi
Gardens like pieces of feathery soot.

In monsoon, an owl in your chest suits you.
Someone has set it on fire again.

It calls and calls, a crawling log.
Turning with termites, wood chips on your porch

are drops of cow dung expanding in rain.
Each morning pilgrims herd to the river.

Each morning you see them at the bathing ghats,
and your wife returns with bits of ash

in her hair when she sits downwind
from Harishchandra Ghat, the crematorium.

Everything in the world is supposed to
pour through everything else. You could die

in Banaras and wake in the wood ibis
in the river and no one would know

but the doams, maybe, who rake ash through Ganga.
But what if you don't? What if you sleep instead

for a thousand years, a thousand insults,
kisses, clutchings, a thousand discoveries:

the wheel, fire, phonograph, chainsaw, go-cart,
Saran Wrap, telescope, Tabasco, paint

thinner, martini, artificial heart,
logarithm, aspirin? What if you sleep

in an airtight black space no larger than
a thumb? Living, the doams know, is dying.

Each rake prong digs deeper into river silt.
Each back pang is the death of a stranger.

You could sleep and sleep and the world would go on
without you, but a world without your voice

would be a little less green, a bit
less black, a touch less white. You could die

in Banaras monsoon and no one would know.
The wood ibis in the river wouldn't even know

but might be stunned with the sudden pouring
of light as it lifts its wings in mist toward shore.

A THEORY OF THE FUNCTION OF
THE CONFUSION OF THINGS

"Can't one prove the function of the confusion of things"
—Yoshioka Minoru
(trans. Hiroaki Sato)

You die suddenly one afternoon on a dusty street
in Chowk, confused from the heat

in old town Banaras. A pan dealer sighs
into your death, discovers a lack of water

left you empty as a child's balloon
without air. She peers into afternoon sun

wavering in the vacancy of your eyes, and the hang
in the hem of her faded-green sari calls

the stare of a vulture down from its perch
above a portrait of Mother Kali

who dances on the chest of her prostrate
husband, Shiva, fifty human skulls dangling

from her neck, a girdle of human arms
at her waist. A rickshaw wallah swerves

to avoid your corpse, circles back and pronams
as if dead you are some living god. Now the vulture

comes to investigate. Soldiers circle, propping
their rifles in a row, making a black-metallic fence.

Each one kneels before you briefly, whispers in turn
a secret mantra inside your right ear. *If he could*

*only hear a floating of **OM**, they say, he might return*
to us, descend back to earth in a sudden flutter, avoiding

the frozen movements of the north. Cold winds come
from border skirmishes in Jammu and Kashmir,

from genocide in Tibet, from dark caves of yogis
in the Himalayas whose chanting keeps the earth's

axis moving toward love no matter what
weather might confute the once-opened arms

of strangers who hunch now and huddle, alone,
for warmth. Even from the hem of a woman's green sari

that lightens the stance of an ibis wading
several meters away in the river. She bends

over you, puts a mirror to your mouth, inserts
aniseed into your nostrils, calls the coroner

to complete the certificate with, *Died in Chowk
in afternoon heat, function questionable, species unknown.*

Can a function *be* a function if it is questionable?
A theory of confusion, orderly or just a conglutination

of feather, clothing, and bone?
Her green threads lift like sparrows

in search of brown paint. The wind drops. A broken fence
of vultures circles above you, something almost

round. A vendor selling rudraksha beads
ties your hands together in prayer.

They place a gold coin on your eye, take you down
to the river for twenty rupees to be burned. *This is*

where the great ones like Lahiri Mahasaya lit,
you think, hovering now, a little,

above your corpse at Manikarnika Ghat. Centuries of saints
leaving earth as flares. Centuries, too, of the unknown

like yourself mixing flesh and fire
to ash. Centuries of seeds

planted in river-bottom mud and flourishing years
later as a sadhu in holy Hardwar, a computer

analyst in Eureka, California, a cowboy
on the outskirts of Buenos Aires, a flea in the fur

of a Mongolian pony, some swatch of dust
above an Indiana doorway. You feel your skin begin

to burn, the fragment of time called *Me*
drop away, Mother Ganga clock through

your no-longer-ticking heart. For hours and hours,
rich volcanic lapse spins black butterflies

that catch the Banaras breeze like bits
of burnt air, that settle tiny birds

into the hair of a passing stranger, in the dhoti
folds of a pilgrim with brass bowl, that bathe

the banks of this most holy river
with the dark light of your death.

KARMIC SEEDS

The mind may move toward anything white,
but Nilakantha's throat is blue from drinking

poison that would have destroyed the world.
A rickshaw wallah may see a bent wheel

as a day's lost wage, but a Rajput king
might have seen a bent sword as salvation.

A politician embarks on a padyatra,
traveling from village to village for support,

and the force with which he pronams local
dignitaries sends power through the lines

to light a bulb that has been out six months
in a sari shop on the outskirts of town.

You consider the curve of the world, lines
of thought one scatters as seeds that sprout

good marks in sixth-grade math, a flat tire
on the way to work, arriving just in time

for the last loaf of bread, rain for the family
reunion, thinking of a caterpillar

and suddenly spotting a butterfly
on a gravel road at dusk. You wonder

about the karma you have accumulated
these past forty years. *It takes so long,*

you think, *for anything to grow. It's a shame
for it all to dissolve when you die.* Or

does it dissolve? A person may react
negatively to another despite

his best intentions. He may say each morning
with conviction, *Today will be different, today I will give*

unconditional love, and yet when the soup arrives cold,
uncontrollably scolds the waiter,

bunching his napkin abruptly into a ball.
He may break off his conversation, unknowingly,

with a friend, forgetting to detail that part
of last night's dream where he brought a horse

into his home and dressed it in baby clothes.
He may spot a cigarette from the corner

and remember being rocked as an infant
of an aboriginal tribe before a fire in Orissa

just before the coming of the British
Raj. He may feel heat at the Sun Temple

at Konarak, touch stone-carved chariots,
and suddenly recall the weight of the wheel

of a Conestoga in Oregon
crossing the diamonds of his back

and slashing his rattlesnake head.
He may put on his father's shirt and feel

that buttons on the right are wrong. He may
insist upon buttoning it from the bottom

up, agonizing at the tails, wondering
why each time before he begins

an image of an unknown woman
in an elevator in 1920s Paris,

pheasant feather stuck in her hat, suddenly
comes to him, falling seven floors

to her death when the lower end of the cable—
without any warning—frays and snaps.

He may develop a rash on his left forearm
and remember centuries before

competing with other amoebas for water.
He may wonder why each struggling drop

of sperm in a condom makes him weep in his wife's
arms with the thought of genocide in Tibet.

Where does it end, this coming back and back?
Or perhaps, why *should* it end? Your rickshaw

wallah knows the imperative of a round
wheel, knows that only with each turn

does his family get fed. If it wasn't for monsoon,
you think, you'd probably be dead by now

from the heat in Uttar Pradesh.
Shiva might not have wanted to be Nilakantha,

might not have wanted his throat the color
blue, but a moment of pure love isn't

always pure, isn't necessarily
white, might bring with the touch or tongue

of another all the struggles of their many lives,
their healings, hurts, seeds.

A Rajput king might have once ruled
with a beautiful curved sword,

and a silk weaver in Rajasthan
three centuries later might develop

curvature of the spine, hunched over
his loom with dye in his mouth, holding his shuttle

like a tiny wooden knife that cuts color
crosswise into thread, into the pattern

of a striped shirt someone might wear—in Copenhagen
or Topeka—calling it his own.

A THEORY OF THE ORIGIN OF BIRTH

When did you want it, need it, orbits of skin on fingers
and thumbs keeping you from stars, locked in human touch?

When did you ask for it, need it, the crawling out
into moist reptilian night for frog skin and splendor?

When did you desire the breast as a moment of growing
bones? As countless moments of your growing bone?

You examine a mango at the Lanka market and know the orange
fluid pours back through you in secret while you sleep.

You watch a lizard eat a roach the size of a fist
and know the table pounding and head holding must stop.

You see a gravel raker's left breast fall untucked from her sari
and recall the press of silk upon your chest.

You never asked for the stirring of mosquitoes upon the bed
net. The hunger for butter, blood, for a milky moon.

You never asked for a stinging of lanterns. For a field
of lightning bugs swallowing moments of their own light.

You step out onto the verandah, see that Sagittarius
has become an argument over a corpse at a burning ghat.

When did you ask for it? The juice of the mango
mapping your blood with star charts of desire?

The sound sleep, that dream of a frog carried to the ghat
and burned for impersonating Napoleon Bonaparte?

Its smoke over the Ganges, turning into an outline of Gandhi
blessing the Republic with a pail of burnt stars in his hand?

The long herds of pilgrims rustling down to the river
for their mud baths in ashes, sediment, and silt?

The mewlings, the incessant biting of flies. Indian sun
pounding its fruit. Your bedclothes damp and bruised?

NEXT YEAR WHEN I FISH HYDRATES
IN FISCAL BLUE

She bends near the storefront in Poona,
examines sapphire, ruby, hyalite. Her dark

umbrella, half-open, a star
collapsed among sparks. You feel

that scar in your spine, are back in Banaras
with Yogi Raj, eating dal off a banana leaf

plate. No. You are in Poona in August, enduring
monsoon, dipping into your pocket for eggs,

crayons, braids, anything remotely blue
to calm the sky. You are enduring monsoon,

a hydrographer whose hut is flooded with Mula River
moonlight, carp snag clotting the straw. Black

plastic sags in mud, tarps
that part of your heart

you may never know. *Do you weep
because it rains*, the yogi had asked, *or*

do your tears prod the clouds?
You may never know why

she browses jewels, interested only
in amethyst. Why a cow nudges lichi rinds

that contain strains of evening
amber near your wife's feet. Why you want

the Rajasthani bracelet as a silver snake
around your wrist. Suddenly require its scales

in your blood. *More,* uncurls
from something long and pleading.

From childhood praise in first-grade
English, from a paring knife

cut on your left index finger,
an organ lesson half-learned

except for the black keys
of a bruise. From killing that snake on the hill

with a hoe for your mother when you were twelve,
as if you were Saint George, later

grieving for the eggs. You want *more* food, need
more books, require *more* touch, demand *more* milk.

This morning, at sleep's steep, you heard the peepal
tree inhabit the rain's weight, mouth a confusion of sound

that resembled, *Next year when I fish hydrates in fiscal blue.*
Yes, *when I fish hydrates* is not a television game show,

nor a type of wrestling hold, nor a dissolving
vowel, a koan reassembling hips that grind into you

in bed when you crave juice, sense the morning blood
rush ahead and stir the sheet, when the pulp

refuses to flush and you stand there
remembering the shredding apart

when you were twelve. When you wonder why
your father never phoned. How the hill, the imaginary,

the horse, how belly-burn and star, how possibly the scar,
why you ever sold the aquarium, never changed

the charcoal in the first place.
You have come too far, you know,

to coax a home from a flap of black
plastic. But what would leaving

leave you with but dead fish, or cornflower
blue striped in scales of saffron

noon, or a reaching into your pocket and finding
only an egg? That bothers you. The blue cord

at your throat disturbs. Simplicity of care,
coil-brown of sad. The blue-tongued bauxite wagging

that will not stop, will not compress desire to Krishna-
blue, crayon to Baul braid. Malaria to Maloprim,

cholera-green to cassava root. Opal to carp-
snag monsoon. She examines stones,

dangles her umbrella, a half-eaten truffle,
fungus of a fourteenth rib, and now *you're* the one

fixated on buying a lamp? You feel the weight
of the sheet each morning press your penis,

a corpse culling light from camphor rose.
Like lying on a hill, handle of a hoe,

substituting phonics for sex.
You mouth the now of the sitar

you bought in Banaras. May never
learn to control the drone

but reach for more, need the tightening
string, seasoned teak and screw. *Next year*

when I fish hydrates in fiscal blue?
you ask in chants so soft

your heart hardly eats. The snake
will shed its eelgrass slip,

becoming neither grass nor eel, crayon
nor erotic braid, organ lesson nor the half-learned

fardel of fishbowl muck that scales
your spine with bent bones of a throat. Only

a thread-like current, Krishna-blue, to wash your spine
river brown to vowel, to crawl the tongue back

through the casings, cracks, and juice.
To flood the field and go forehead to your egg.

DRINKING TEA AT A SILK SHOP
DURING MONSOON WITH SONS OF
AN INDEPENDENCE FIGHTER

Now the shop swells with passersby
who park rickshaws and carts to dodge
gusts and drink tea with the Westerner
who wants a saffron kurta and pajama,
to learn from some son or other
the origin of free market fruit
in their rotting cart, tales of cleanly cut skulls
of coconuts from Mysore, the way an Asian
pear spilled open in the '40s
into two uneven halves whose seed fed flies.
To speak your mind back then was treason,
the eldest brother says, glancing downward,
then pronaming to a photo. *But father wore
his Gandhi cap with pride,* adds the youngest,
and made us who we are.

                    You sip the silk shop
tea, waiting out monsoon suddenly
thrust upon Banaras like birth-
bag flush. The owners still you
with stories. Their father, a freedom fighter
during Independence. Roping marigolds
almost bring blood to his black and white photo.
They bow to his passing, talk of jails, beatings,
worms in his stool, even Mahatma Gandhi
making salt against regulation
at the Bay of Bengal to show the British
how a skinny Hindu could hold the ocean
in his hand.

          You consider Partition,
atrocities in the Punjab, wonder how
different they are than the daily struggle

back home for bread: drive-bys, maimings,
rape. You touch years of silk in narrow berths
around the walls, consider the coarse fabric
you've brought along, have clung to even after months
of heat, wonder how you've worn it
so long and why, sip tea, and taste the passing
of the British, still, in afternoons
like this that swell a sore within
the city.

       The crowd watches
you closely, waggling heads when you ask
about rain, when the pounding might stop.
They smile, gentle your attempt at Hindi.
One man glances at his friend, tightens
his fist, then rubs his heart three times as if to ask
forgiveness of himself for some secret
knife he thought, a moment, into your
try at tongue. How different shops are
here on the other side of the earth,
or how different you've become? Open palms
having followed you lane to lane,
fester a sore—you're certain—decades
of the Raj sunk into bones of a well?

You've never spent hours sipping tea
on a wood floor among the slash
of Ganges in riverous streets. Never
allowed the afternoon. Never
shopped as if seeking something fluid
from a room of strangers, as if asking
the flood to finally wash everything
away and be your mother. Never

bought pants as a way of seeding
the past, unless it was to dress like your grandfathers
from Greece—Giorgos and Pericles,
blue trouser pleats of the '20s
holding waves of the Ionian
even in Chicago, even within
their bowing at the table after work
before the *baklava* of Helen and Stavroula.
Never heard the birth bag each evening
burst and the moment of pain begin.

You've read the certificate that assures
your breathing came through each of them
on December 3 at precisely
6:18 p.m. You've seen the plastic tag
that cut your name as separate from others
that night who wailed. Felt the invisible
tourniquet as your wrist began to grow,
your mother's milk going moist to bone. Monsoon
stiffens those who've fractured before you
into dust, salt, cup shards, worms, coconut
threads, an Asian pear, even silk. A woman
and screaming infant hunch by. Tiny fists
beat back the drench. You know your skeleton sculpts you
as an instant of distinct rain. You know your bones
separate you from monsoon, from flood,
from the Raj and decades of knife-thrust
and scimitar-slash that coagulate
in the scab of a single tiny reaching. You know
the birth-bag thrust as sin and how your skin
has kept you from your mother's blood.

SCALES OF MOTHER GANGA

Toward the south of holy Banaras,
an old woman rubs open sores

on her left arm, goes in and out
of Durga Temple as if some hidden turnstile

keeps drawing her. Gold carp
flock the pool just north

at the Aghori ashram—
where it is said the sick can bathe

away sin—then breed beneath green
scum, laying an egg that refuses

to hatch except during full moon.
The sun rises from the haze, a river

sore the outline of a bird
crosses, a struggling amoeba. A dead cow,

pale and bloated, somehow makes the river
lighter. *The blood of work weighs less when it is cold.*

You extend your arms and legs, practice the *Cobra.*
Recall those yogis who perform austerities,

the ek-bahu Baba who hasn't dropped
his right arm in twelve years, the sag of his skin,

a dried udder, the man a decaying
tree, one thinned branch about to snap.

Loss can make us heal? Is necessary, even, as we move
toward wholeness? We aren't already whole?

Yesterday, the rickshaw wallah's stance
measured your step, made you

imagine his wife and children.
Such a loving woman, you thought,

surely three lovely sons. Can't ever do enough
to please him. Can't lighten that bruise

on his left calf, the one you glimpsed that
rubbed the bicycle seat when he stood to pump you

up a hill in 115-degree heat. You gave him
an extra five rupees, barely sixteen cents. He took it,

looked away into road dust, wore his incapacity
to love his family back like an invisible shirt.

He is unable to love, or you
have made him empty as you fill

your senses with the strange sights
of Banaras? With the need to read

about religion at the university
library? A single-celled organism

can even love, as it thinks itself
into a morphic field, grows into a slab

of granite, a parasite, a hibiscus flower, a gold carp,
cobra, cow, a man, woman, a Himalayan yogi

who learns to no longer breathe. Each loss
is a way to score a forearm, to step into thick green

scum, dipping brass into a pool
looking for a fish egg? Each thinned arm,

a lifting toward what you might become,
or what you already are? You don't want

to ride the bruise on a rickshaw wallah's
calf. You don't want to taste

the snake of your lie. You want him
to go home, play with his sons, hold his wife, tell her

she's pretty, eat paneer, conceive a daughter,
love her for the son she is not.

The sun rides the haze, a cell of saffron
you might enter if you would but bathe in the river.

HUM
OF
THE
WORLD

A TEMPLE POOL MIGHT IGNITE
(Lotus-Blood from Your Heart)

Not the wind in your hair but dying
carp. Each curl a curving inward
toward some damp sound. You ride the rickshaw
like finally getting even. You dream
you murdered the young man with too many
turn-left-here's and *stop-now-there's*, and felt
your life had closed. All night those spokes
had followed you to tea stalls, lassi stands,
even to the mirror you refused
to kiss. Why do you wake
each morning craving jack fruit, the bed-
sheet still raised several inches stiffly
above your waist? The wheel turns and turns.
Blood rushes to the open wound.
Empty spoke spaces shadow your thoughts?
Salt-blotched rubber thongs on a stranger's feet
are an unwound turban on a bed of nails?
It's a question of controlling your
passion, the yogi told you over and again
with his eyes, chanting some strand of sound
all the way from the *Bhagavad-Gita*
down into fruit pits dried as beads
in his hands. If the stirring in your groin
was rotating lotus light, a temple pool
might finally ignite from pure, gold
gill-fire. If could swallow the fin-flash
of Kali's sword, pike Shiva's trident
as hooks in your heart, the bleeding might stop.

GOLD CARP JACK FRUIT MIRRORS

1. Gold Carp

You want, simply, to stop breathing and hear.
Yesterday was a day just like tomorrow.

A sun window, carved in a narrow cave,
pulls light onto a small Buddhist stupa.

Dust above a Kashi doorway is cornmeal
in the bowl of a wandering sadhu.

Picasso soup! I ordered Picasso soup!
What else is there but a solid hammer?

If you breathe cords of bees in your navel,
upward toward your throat, you will see blue light

flutter a hummingbird in your forehead.
In Banaras heat you don't want Pepsi.

You only want the juice of the jack fruit.
Liquid stones! Liquid stones! Liquid stones!

the sadhu suddenly cries in samadhi.
You finally get out, a kilometer

from your destination, hoping for food.
Heat lightning in the lines is a traveling

of the inner topography of a snail.
A swallowtail drifts in fierce Banaras

sun, *Don't you yet see, I am your own?*
Tired, you wish that you could stop wishing.

Walking in Kashi, you feel in each cell
the hum of the world from fruit stalls,

flower sellers, rickshaws, marigold bees.
Children piss in the still green water

of Ganga that has run down from heaven,
cushioned by Shiva's wild, matted hair.

A baby monkey clings to its mother,
hissing at passersby at the Temple

of Shitala Devi near Chousatti Ghat.
Joan Miro was not Paul Klee! Not even

the gathering of bees or the ink of squids!
What might you touch but solidified sound

in the shape of a wall, a piece of celery,
a ceiling, a cloud, a martini,

a lover's tongue, eighty-five cents left in rupees
on the table by the people before you?

Today, all you see is a bucket
of ash emptied onto the shore.

Paul Klee was not a caterpillar!
Carp come to still temple water out of nowhere.

Breaking words like slicing a coconut.
Christ and Krishna have the same

etymological root, the same tuft of sound.
The most sacred Indian art

has a dimension of guided eros.
Migratory finches and aboriginal bees.

How far do they travel to find sound?
You want to be in the cauldron, a black

bean, a piece of parsley, the gold carp
tasting swallows of a temple pool in Sarnath.

If you could but feel orbits of love pressed
into your forehead on a thumbprint.

You want the warmth of the opening meal
cooking slowly over a morning fire.

Jack fruit falling to earth as jack fruit.
There are many myths about the sexual

prowess of those who were tigers in former lives.
Most maps are wrong, the sadhu says, *the way*

to the heart is the way to the heart.
Back home, the mouth of a corpse is sown shut

to prevent any leakage of the words of death.
A mango falling to earth as moon.

The white hump of a Brahma bull
is a clot of moonlight working its way

down through straw ceilings and dung-clad walls,
through a worm crawling on carrots in the corner.

There is a moment when all moments collide,
the peepal tree bends in Banaras breeze.

All the sins of one's previous births are destroyed
as soon as one enters the boundaries

of Kashi, Lord Shiva told Parvati.
This tree, yes, this tree, yes—no, not this tree.

The silence of the world is a fishbone.
A brussels sprout in the turn of a young girl's hoop.

2. Jack Fruit

Jack fruit falling to earth as jack fruit.
Walking in Kashi, you feel in each cell

the hum of the world from fruit stalls,
flower sellers, rickshaws, marigold bees.

A baby monkey clings to its mother,
hissing at passersby at the Temple

of Shitala Devi near Chousatti Ghat.
Most maps are wrong, the sadhu says, *the way*

to the heart is the way to the heart.
A swallowtail drifts in fierce Banaras

sun, *Don't you yet see, I am your own?*
All the sins of one's previous births are destroyed

as soon as one enters the boundaries
of Kashi, Lord Shiva told Parvati.

If you could but feel orbits of love pressed
into your forehead on a thumbprint.

You want to be in the cauldron, a black
bean, a piece of parsley, the gold carp

tasting swallows of a temple pool in Sarnath.
The most sacred Indian art

has a dimension of guided eros.
There are many myths about the sexual

prowess of those who were tigers in former lives.
The silence of the world is a fishbone.

Yesterday was a day just like tomorrow.
Breaking words like slicing a coconut.

What else is there but a solid hammer?
Liquid stones! Liquid stones! Liquid stones!

the sadhu suddenly cries in samadhi.
Picasso soup! I ordered Picasso soup!

Dust above a Kashi doorway is cornmeal
in the bowl of a wandering sadhu.

Migratory finches and aboriginal bees.
How far do they travel to find sound?

In Banaras heat you don't want Pepsi.
You only want the juice of the jack fruit.

Back home, the mouth of a corpse is sown shut
to prevent any leakage of the words of death.

A mango falling to the earth as moon.
Children piss in the still green water

of Ganga that has run down from heaven,
cushioned by Shiva's wild, matted hair.

A brussels sprout in the turn of a young girl's hoop.
Tired, you wish that you could stop wishing.

The white hump on the back of a Brahma bull
is a clot of moonlight working its way

down through straw ceilings and dung-clad walls,
through a worm crawling on carrots in the corner.

Paul Klee was not a caterpillar!
Carp come to still temple water out of nowhere.

Today, all you see is a bucket
of ash emptied onto the shore.

Joan Miro was not Paul Klee! Not even
the gathering of bees or the ink of squids!

If you breathe cords of bees in your navel,
upward toward your throat, you will see blue light

flutter a hummingbird in your forehead.
You finally get out, a kilometer

from your destination, hoping for food.
You want, simply, to stop breathing and hear.

What might you touch but solidified sound
in the shape of a wall, a piece of celery,

a ceiling, a cloud, a martini,
a lover's tongue, eighty-five cents left in rupees

on the table by the people before you?
There is a moment when all moments collide,

the peepal tree bends in Banaras breeze.
Heat lightning in the lines is a traveling

of the inner topography of a snail.
A sun window, carved in a narrow cave,

pulls light onto a small Buddhist stupa.
Christ and Krishna have the same

etymological root, the same tuft of sound.
You want the warmth of the opening meal

cooking slowly over a morning fire.
This tree, yes, this tree, yes—no, not this tree.

GETTING
THE
TONGUING
TENDER
ENOUGH

MEETING ALISON AT THE MALAVIYA BHAVAN, BANARAS HINDU UNIVERSITY

You meet at the Yoga Institute,
and then. And then, and always,
and maybe. Maybe there's some purpose
for blonde hair tied in a bun
today, after a month of sensing the remoteness
of your brown curls amidst so much glistening
black. Maybe there's a reason
the teacher's late, that you're the only two
except for the water buffalo that has wandered
into the court looking for shade, that
you're sweating through blue denim hearing
her stories of inoculations and premature
labor and rabies and the birthing of goats
in a hut with forceps meant for villagers.
Maybe there's hope that she's a doctor,
about your age, and from England, Leeds
in fact, about which you know absolutely nothing
yet feel you do because your second favorite Who album
was cut live there in '70. And *Summertime Blues*
is precisely what you've got, and for which
Roger Daltry keeps wailing, *there ain't no cure.*

So maybe it's destiny that you meet
the blonde doctor from Leeds today
when you thought you were over culture
shock and the desire to touch
anything remotely English. Your wife
and you collapsed beneath mosquito netting
just yesterday at three when the power again went out
and the air conditioner groaned
like a drowning cat and 122
felt not like electrocution
but death by sweat. You tried to joke
that your *Lonely Planet* guidebook

couldn't have picked a better name if it had tried,
but it was a lie. *Alison*, she tells you,
as if stepping out of the cool smoky blue
of that Elvis Costello song—*Alison (my aim is true)*—
extending her thin hand
like some pale strong bird, some rare
parakeet that you fear
you could crush if you shook
with what you were really feeling. Not fear.
Not loneliness, exactly. Not love. Not even
lust. But the pain of living
so close to what you always wanted
and so far from how it actually feels.

She says she forgot her water, asking
for maybe a sip. In this heat, you think,
she might just as well have closed the body,
suddenly realizing she'd replaced someone's kidney
with a clock. Which might not
be a bad idea if you wanted to track
the passing of snow geese through mineral deposits
of history, the tick tick tick of a migratory
stone bringing on queasiness, or the way
Phoenician yeast competes with Greek cheese
for the focus of the plate, or even that curve you take
for work back home when you're late
and you wonder why you always go a little
too fast. You hesitate, considering cholera,
typhoid, meningitis, dysentery,
hepatitis—that litany of diseases
that your inoculants only partially protect
you from, the roll call your guidebook bugles
out then flags as taps over your stay,
how even the American CDC warns against
getting too close. But you give her some of yours

anyway, boiled by your wife this morning
over a propane stove like fresh blood
panned and washed from the river,
shaken loose from gravel and dirt, from
the pumping forth and arterial lift
of your daily bread. She drinks Indian
style, without touching lip to rim, the bottle
at least four inches above her upturned mouth,
eyes shut. A blind bird
fed a fat wiggly worm,
she knows each coiling drop
and how it will fall. The way jungle rain comes
great distances from mangroves to broad-leafed rubber
plants all the way down to bones, needles, and silt.

You're relieved. You had hesitated
when she asked, knowing she'd been nine months
in villages with nothing but well water,
goat shit, and human piss. Yet
you're sad now to take the bottle back
and not tongue the slight quiver
of her question, taste the rim sweat
of new lips, the first wails of infants
in huts you're certain she carries, the labor of her
staying alive amidst cholera and typhoid and goats,
and strength of listening to the tick tick tick of so many
human hearts, which is enough itself
to kill anyone. Those lips which are lovely.
But of which you know absolutely nothing
except that she's from Leeds and textiles
and doesn't really like The Who and doesn't seem
that blue anyway and, oh, you're married.

You wait together in the comfortable silence
of those who have touched. Of those who smoke

afterwards in the quiet glow and know
they'll touch again, even if they don't but will
only maybe in dream. You wait for the man
with the keys, for Dr. Banerjee,
for his lecture at the Bhavan
about the transformation of human salt,
about the yeast catching on
even through the thunderstorms
of our lives. You wait for note taking
and questions and, oh, how she might sit
four inches from you and hold her pen
in her left hand with awkward purpose. Will she
scribble like a physician? Will her notes be
decoded only by those who pour potions
and pills? Will you meet again, so she can
borrow your bottle and without stethoscope
listen closely to the drip drip drip
of your heart? Will you find yourself
scouring desk tops, book covers, secret palms,
for her scrawl in India ink,
for her diagnosis of why we suffer
and how to finally fix things
and make it right? Will she teach you
how to cock your arm and work your lips
so that what passes between you
will remain forever clean, suspended
in air like a great untouched waterfall?
Like a moment of boiled untapped power,
begun at home at the propane by your wife,
almost withheld, yet given at the last instant
out of compassion or loneliness or clutch,
and then, and always, and maybe?

AS YOU BREATHE IN THE SLOUCHING

In this city of tombs, you feel incredibly alive.
And all your past, the kisses, the defeats.

Even the clutching in the dark. Where are they now?
The Mogul tomb is a brown river moon thrust up into light.

You see the tomb and feel a scrag of the Jamuna River.
Listen: one carp plus one carp always equals one gold carp.

Brilliantly, trees are swimming through afternoon Delhi sky.
All that blue remains as only an outline for peepal leaves.

You stepped out of one moon and entered another.
And everyone else believes that they cannot fly?

Not everyone, you realize, as you breathe in the slouching
of those who swat mosquitoes and fear their next life.

Malaria now, or some later incarnation as a pig?
One death plus one death is said to equal a jar of Bombay Gin.

One mosquito net above the bed is enough to culch the moon
of all its waste, drag the river for minnow scum and shad.

Not always, you realize, as you drink in Lodi Gardens.
Blue peacock fire blazing the glaze of sun on red sandstone.

And all your past, the sorrowful kisses, the joyous defeats?
All that glorious death, and you're still alive.

AT RED FORT

Here the Mogul emperor rode out on
elephant back into the streets of old

Delhi. Red sandstone walls of Lal Quila
still hold blood of both Muslims and Hindus.

The fourteenth son, Aurangzeb, deposed his
father and imprisoned him in Agra Fort,

forcing him to contemplate empty coffers
and his wife's tomb, the Taj Mahal.

So this son was the first and last to drink these
sun-cliff walls, kiss moonlight in the breasts

of his many wives beneath bulbous domes
and towering minarets, eat racked lamb

and clap for dancing, tossing bones to dogs.
So he was the last of the great Moguls,

though there were more—up to the Mutiny
when the British retook Delhi a few

meters from here at bloody Kashmir Gate—
and the tongue of his faith tossed temples down

like bits of cardamom seed picked from teeth
after tea and built mosques with domes that rose

from temple brick like magnificent mouths.
For 100 rupees you get a tour

from a boy who makes his living talking English
to strangers. How many Moguls, British,

and Hindus died here is unknown,
and what the boy says may or may not be true.

He talks and talks and all you want to do
is feel a moment of many lives die

inside to teach you what and what not
to eat and drink: rack of lamb and curry,

chips of flint and sword-cut in red walls,
a national anthem muffled in a bowl

of mulligatawny, the milk of nine
glorious orgasms one night beneath the full moon

of many breasts, authentic sandstone
and a glass of beet juice you're offered at the gate.

AT THE TAJ MAHAL

A moth lifts the Saturn shift
in your pupil, milk of an Agra goat

milting in your groin. Add sea-salt at a stall
to chickpeas and dal and hear the Jamuna River

scrape scrotal pearls of Mogul dead
below the Taj Mahal. In Banaras,

at the ashram of the Aghoris, you learned
of Baba Kina Ram taming bats, crawling

the sixteenth-century darkness down. They covered him
in scales until he commanded them to the tamarind

where their ancestors still hang. Tantric heat
let loose from his cave, lightning

cords from his spine. You touched
the feet of his disciple, Darshananda,

ate the sacred mango, its pulp later that night
thinning to empty black, felt fever-drench,

jolts of dehydration. Was it cholera
you feared? Dysentery? A moment too pure

for your core, pressing nerve ganglia
with clags of divine light? Your born-again-

Christian guide, Rhagavan, having also touched
those feet, having eaten from that same mango,

cried out across town in his own moment
near death, *Lord Jesus Christ, have mercy on me!*

How two months later in Agra a luna moth
spreads the opium green velvet of its wing, drags

darkness down from a tamarind, tangent
of soot and jewel-looting from the Taj.

Cremation ash tans tiny wedges of noon
into night, creases air with the ceasing

of bats. A tug on your left big toe
during yoga practice creates an electrical imbalance

across town in the sari shop during monsoon? Chars afternoon
tea with fennel and a smoldering

bicycle tire in rain? Makes a moth
wing close around a blanch of ash? Encourages

the ectoplasmic migration of eels
near a mausoleum? Cremated curls of a man

who collapsed collecting cup shards for chai
blossom as tile across its floor

in intricate Mogul design. The left wrist of a widow snaps
the inlay twist of twigs. Baba Kina Ram,

having healed a Brahmin's son, tossed rice
grain into Krim Kund, mouthed a mantra,

pronounced, *Whoever would bathe in this water*
for five Tuesdays and Sundays would also be free

from his suffering. You search stalls near the Taj
for clear water, for a mango free of cholera mixed

with light, free of *yes* infused with *no*, the exact moment
of fever—on opposite sides of Banaras—of an American yogi

and Indian Christian. Compare a goat bleat
in an Agra bazaar to the thirst of a face that asks

for baksheesh, even just a rupee for gauze
around the stump that was once this leper's

left hand. You wish it was Sunday or Tuesday
and holy Banaras and Krim Kund

and a perfect circle you might trace from a moth's
velvet into his leprous wrist. But you are here,

and this monomer of death *is* round
as your camera composes its light.

All the travel guides say you must see
this tomb in full moon to clearly catch

its curve. But at noon, beyond the bazaar,
sun cuts back from minaret to eye to the space

where inlaid jewels should be. You see
a massive marble atom at the center of the world,

what you always sensed within
the stir of fruit and word.

EVERY DAY AT THREE

Mohan parks his rickshaw, chews pan to forget the heat.
That's the way it is in Banaras in May.

The dead rise out of the river and bring
their bloated purple wrists through the street.

Look: photons step out of a vacuum tube
and become lichis and Asian pears.

Veterans of the Afghani War meet once a month
at the hall to play cards and recall who won what, when.

The Lalita Cinema and posters preparing for lines
of young men who wait to see an actress's bare shoulders.

Durga Temple's red sandstone and the monkeys who pretend
shyness, then steal eyeglasses of tourists.

You trudge through coffins of dust in Ganga Bag Colony,
hear fruit in your mesh bag begin to bruise.

You must walk the path softly, yet with purpose,
the yogi said, and you believe him.

Mohan waggles his head, spits red betel juice
into afternoon dust, says, *No ride, Baba. Too hot.*

Every day at three, even the pigs in your lane
lie down in a line and forget the trash.

You step around cow droppings, rotting lettuce, stagnant
water, instinctively now, without even looking.

A THEORY OF THE CHOKE OF DUST

Step out onto your lane
at Ganga Bag Colony, feel

the choke of dust as an elephant
dissolving to particles

in your lung, move through mud
you're certain was not there

yesterday, through droppings of water
buffalo whose tails gently swat

the flies. A hornet hive
on the corner house

is a tiny tornado
with something gummy dripping

from its core. A group of boys
hammer wickets into hard

Banaras earth, curse May heat
and why so many have to die

without a chance to play
cricket. A young girl,

absorbed in a cloud
of brown roses,

watches them from her
muddy yard, places paddies

of buffalo dung on her hut,
chanting in hopscotch

rhythm, *In-dya, In-dya.*
They bowl the ball and slap

the bat and hit and miss,
stepping aside for you

to walk by, smirking at your
nervous smile, at the way

you choke on their dust,
hunch in their heat.

ICON

At full moon, you ride the rickshaw
with your wife, bellies momentarily calmed
from the vegetarian thali at the Sindhi,

lean back into torn red vinyl, into the swoosh
of pumping calloused feet, glimpse the river just off
Asi Road trimmed with scales of some snake. Everything

in the world curves around your still
center. You pass Lolark Kund and sense the edge
of centuries around which Banaras grew,

a murky green pool fifty feet
below city stone. Bone chips, coins, broken
bangles claw back through the moon

and lay their people down again to die
upon your lap. A gold carp in green Banaras scum
is a flash of heat lightning across Indiana

sky just before a tornado. Pulls you down again
into thirty-year radio crack and basement candle
swirl in an icon of Saint George. Becomes

ruby sparks in the harness of his horse? You see dogs
at the side of its full white belly, dogs at the side
of this road digging beds in sand and rags. Men and women

crawl up to sleep on a low Banaras wall.
The world of death and heat lie down together
in the almost cool. It's been 122

all day, and now 105 says ice. You exhale
into the moon, somehow taste a wafer
that will not melt, a lost coin, a radio wave

flouncing a massive horse head rounded out
by the dark. It is perfectly quiet,
except for your wife's breath and the concept

of the wheels. You can't imagine ever going home
and you can't stay. That turning which contains the grate
and spoke of your tongue, which constrains you

though somehow smoothes your mood. If the moon
would bruise the temple, strike the sawmill
on Madanpura, the world would expand then contract,

a prodded pupil, spear-slit spark, a sudden
poise of beauty into pain. A murky star
becomes a spur. A woman steps from a curb,

floods a lantern through the dark
rutted road, floats a dust
swirl like a tiny tornado at each wheel,

beneath your rickshaw wallah's foot.
Startles you with the fluent tear of muscle
and crack of his thrust, with the slap

of a rag that binds his heel to the bicycle's squeak,
cinching you to this bed. Makes you cup your eye
and squint off the fire's sudden splash.

CUT OF THE WORLD

All night wondering why you're here,
what you came to find. Something
to do with the bruise. That hole you carry
and get sick of so fill with clotted
cream, or that canker sore you try to cure
even with a tonguing you know
will deepen the sting. Mosquitoes frustrated
with the bed net, as if through some secret order
they've come to know your skin all the way
from the States, now seem confused
to be kept off. But that's the way it is
sometimes. You get pushed away
during an intimacy and realize
it's not the stubble burning her cheek
but the ragged words, the urgent touch
that's either too soon or somehow selfish
and remote. Or you get asked back,
but the hostess's stutter flattens out
and jerks like a sick pulse, inhabits an edge,
deadens the guests with ice crushed into crystal
goblets.

          So you come again
to this net, an edge untucked,
poise of wings and beatings and plots
above you formed from restless breath,
this heat that sends you at midnight
to the verandah of the flat
where it all seems so open
a moment, possibilities of stars
like lanterns prone on slatted
pallets, pigs finally grunting
the great sigh of what seems to them
ice, water buffalo hunkered
cool at last in their mud.

　　　　　　But the cut
of the world is still there
in your own yard, or at least
at its rented edge, ledge of sandstone stuck
by your landlord with broken bottles
of Thumbs Up and Gold Spot, clay
teacup shards displaying the jagged perimeter
slash of lightning as if the red earth will always storm
apart and never be enough, wicked wedges
of mango and lichi jars, recycled
Bowie knives that could take
the finger or kneecap off any intruder.
In the next yard, at least two families sleep
in a room the size of your den
back home. Men, women, and children
appear when stars knock the heat
down a little, climb out to lie on low smooth walls
like exhausted dogs who wait, half-alert,
for someone to return, unsure who
it might be, or if, or when.
Sunken into that underwater
twitch of paw, those submarine-sound
pleasure yelps. Yet their shifting alert enough
to snatch a falling bone
or wag a tail and soften
an ear if someone
were finally to arrive.

　　　　　　You're shy
to look, have closed the amber-tinted glass
between you before, afternoons
when you've changed,
but now watch restless
sleep, their almost-satisfied breath
like after making love. You lie

in the lantern spill of hay,
and wonder if it was lust
or the desire for love that drove you
to that shudder, that almost-stinging
moment, then the momentary glow
of ash before it is blown out
from above, or below, or from wherever
that great stirring begins.
That brought you to the knife point
that makes the clotting come
later when you lazily swat a mosquito,
but it's already sunk its pledge
unseen below skin.

                  Like trawling
for tonic town to town, trying
to drain a rash with a wagon rut
and hose. Or carrying an empty mug
between rooms, arguing virtues
of coffee, mango pulp, or milk. Craving only milk
and its bond of bone growth, hay glow,
and moon, yet knowing it's the caffeine jolt
of trying to love, of wondering why
you've come all this way, that stuns
entire families to crawl out their heat
and shift their intimate sleep
before you on a starlit ledge. That disturbs
the lip of a rented wall slicing off the rest
with sharp stars of Gold Spot and Thumbs Up.
That draws the cut out of its bed
onto the verandah, manic for salve or air.

AT THE ASHRAM OF TRAILANGA SWAMI

The temple priest tells you he cannot recollect
being a silk trader nine years ago in Delhi

but can recall every detail of his last incarnation
when he wandered Calcutta as a cow,

vowing never again to nuzzle trash
for cabbage leaves and lichi rinds.

A sweeper woman hunched into a stick
of incense confides with downcast eyes

that she sees God in every ringlet of smoke
but not in the curl of her daughter's hair

nor in the evening lust her husband returns
with, sweaty from river washing,

musk of some Brahmin's shirt
still clinging to him. Does the body

bring one closer to or further
from oneself? The reaching

of a tongue into the salt of another
steady your craving or substitute

moaning for *OM*? Trailanga Swami
taught that the sacred syllable could be heard

in every cell if one could but turn
the tongue toward the nectar

that drips from the back of the throat,
but how can one learn to move from the body

into that sound? Into a temple
pool's luminous flash of carp? Into liquid

flesh, perfect dissolve? You chant a secret
mantra, pour water over the massive Shiva lingam

he retrieved 130 years ago from the bottom
of Ganga, touch its centuries of sexual longing

smooth from the clutch of many hands,
firm from cremation ash spinning electrons black

in your inner ear. Why is it you sometimes hear
a buzzing, get an erection when caressing the rind

of a jack fruit, or when writing a poem
about a leopard, rich underbelly

of ribgrass? You bow to the statue
of the one you've come so far to feel,

the great Trailanga. Dead for 100 years, he vibrates
still in the stone. Mounds of marigolds

flower his neck in fiery ropes, luminous
snakes unwound into higher regions

where sadhus swear a cool wind from below somehow comes
all the way to the throat as Kundalini's hot scales

unwind the spine. 300 pounds of saintliness,
you think, yet gravity could not hold.

All that is moving is still, the temple
priest confides, turning a cabbage leaf

in his left hand, *and all that is still,*
continues. You see a swirling atom

in his finger. Wonder what about being a cow
had left him fixated on lichis. Consider

your own former lives—a monk, perhaps, who wrote poetry
in a fourteenth-century English abbey, an Athonian

Hesychast who tried to love God but touched himself
in private while milking a goat, a wandering sadhu

who, once a year, ate meat and smoked,
a janitor in Alabama, a Tuscaloosa kudzu leaf

blurring this way, that, some insect
or other crucified in the curious fist

of a boy fixed to earth by the name *Georgie*
or *Giorgos* or *Please, take me to your bed*. Something

is always burning and something
is always in heat. Recall the ant

that crossed your desk this morning, certain
it carried your name across its black as it sifted

each poem draft for ash, probing the black
and white photo of a Calcutta yogi

on leopard mat. Its left antenna testing each paw-print
blotch as a hummingbird purls when searching sugar

water. Depth of a lover's tongue
urging spasms of salt, levigating

red and white cells of the beloved
into milky, white divine death.

A THEORY OF THE SHAPE OF PALMS

You take the Deccan Express to Bombay.
You hear the track below as a peacock in your throat.

You had heard that a hundred horses had their throats slit.
The Maharaja had said, *Praise the Lord of All Life!*

And into the Sacred River, blood from the horse sacrifice.
And semen crust thinned out in river washing.

Now the wheels of ten thousand scars
somehow repeat to you who and what you are.

Palm trees in the shape of palm trees.
A dancing bear at the station looking like a dancing bear.

You didn't mean to do it. Truly.
You were just a kid and hadn't known desire

and the space of Indiana oak
could follow you this far.

A woman bends into her chipping of road stone.
Outline of a crack and a bulging of warmth from her sari.

You feel you could finally be saved
in the tucks and tuft of so much tightness.

The bear, the dancing red cap, that gold chain
that will never be home to so much grace and weight.

Newspaper pillows left near the track,
bunched and tumbling out of the station onto the street.

That thrumming in your throat is a hundred slits
invisible at your wrist, still hobbling your heart.

That bending, sweat-outlined buttock, hint of patchouli or
jasmine, and the folds of too much work, too little love.

You consider the British Raj, wonder if spurring the polo ponies
in Calcutta and Delhi was also erotic compassion.

If the lust for full brown thighs thins out
into the Sacred River or actually thins the River itself.

Palm trees in the shape of palms.
A dancing bear looking incredibly like a dancing bear.

A woman chips road stone.
Outline of a crack, outline of a crack.

Not breast nor thigh, you realize. Not even exotic sweat-
scented brown feminine bending, but the star,

that lovely space in your own forehead,
might be egg enough and tuck enough and heat.

THE ATOMIC WEIGHT OF DUSK

A rickshaw wallah in Banaras eats tangerine
rinds and feels stilling dusk

finally quiet the muscles of his thighs.
When he lights a cigarette, a sweeper woman

several kilometers away bends her day
into the river, bringing back flecks of fire

toward the lip of her pot. Even as a hungry child
curled on a hemp cot in a dung hut cups her navel

and contemplates the coming of the Milky Way,
water buffalo might shuffle back from long grass,

udders full, and settle into a dream of dust
and muddy water, a field where every fly bites

only pigs. Does a coming of dusk signal the end
of our lives, or rather the beginnings

of a star forming from random fields of isotopes
and ether, a saffron thread that suddenly falls

fire from the robe of a monk and floats
a hairline crack through the vaporous space

between afternoon and night? Does the atomic weight
of ruthenium ever equal the valence of salt?

The even measure of starlight on Mars?
The boiling point of human blood? In Calcutta,

diesel fumes burn your eyes and rustle
palms. A poet complains of headaches,

presses her chest, and stays the day
smoking in her bathrobe, hears honking buses

and cars as inner music that she says heals
the broken part of her marriage. The rut

of an abandoned rickshaw wheel
can still be felt in ten thousand flowers

exiled as scars. Even as a forty-eight-
year-old woman refuses to be photographed

and bends instead into the glow
of her cigarette, ash begins the slow ascent.

There is a dark tunnel of unknowing, the sadhu
at Dakshineswar told you at river's edge,

*that we must nonetheless walk
as lamps.* A teenage girl

with a red glowing planet on her forehead
suddenly steps out of evening mist and Calcutta fumes,

startles you with open hand and the press of her need,
offers you sparks of light in a garland of marigolds.

GETTING THE TONGUING TENDER ENOUGH

One of those moments you know
cannot last forever. And shouldn't,
though the ice sculpture of the elephant
god begins to slowly grieve itself to heat.
People from all over arrive in their finest,
the hotel courtyard beginning to brim and stretch,
a balloon pressed from both sides.
And your hands, both of them, holding
the shade from your second floor
room so you see, your wife
sprawled on the bed behind you, overcome
by the heat. How 115 wasn't enough
to keep them away, like flies following
those six water buffalo each day to the Ganges
to bite them a little in their moment
of water and remind them of the pain granted
to both the small and the large, to hover
above their heads and buzz,
that extra chakra, the seventh,
only a few might enter if they could
just get the tonguing tender enough.

So the wedding might begin, the gates
are closed and all the bright clothes
shine: saris, kurtas, Banaras silk. Yellows radiant
as cholera in relief, reds like sunsets
tugging salve from sunburnt skin, purples
so bright you think the bruise of the world
was finally beat out into violet. And the busboy, Kumar,
fanning his sculpture, working to keep the good fortune
of Ganesh cool at least until bride and groom arrive.
Which they finally do, though separately,
after blessing hours of cobblestone
and narrow, winding lanes by palanquin and great shoulders
that say, *You can lean on me but only for a while
before the aching begins.* Making their parents collapse

into the pressure of tradition, fathers all over the world
extending chests like colorful birds about to mate, mothers
struggling with tears so their makeup won't run
and ruin the shade they've chosen
to say how happy they really are, though this leaving
leaves them stunned awhile until they discover
the next move and make it right. All the warm breath
building in the open court, the intricate peacock steps
around the marriage fire, vows, stolen
soulful looks, the looking away, the exchange
about *forever* and *health* and *sickness* and *death*
that in any language, and however danced, sends a shudder,
the sudden lance of an ice cream headache,
throughout the crowd, a shudder as if hit
by a brick, by many bricks
that collapse from the past to tell you
how not to build too permanent a home.

Then the jewels and gold are shown, given
for neck, ears, fingers, toes, wrists.
Rings that affirm the family circle. Pearls
that expand friendship into the intimate strand.
Toe rings that touch the bride
where the groom might go. Bangles thin
and gold as a moment of heat lightning pouring
at the pulse, passed all evening with great pleasure
from bridal wrist to eye to heart. Ruby-studded
hand flowers grasping slender fingers,
skin dye of the bride in delicate jasmine
design beneath—clasped and reclasped,
admired and almost smelled during the dancing
and pronams and sweetmeats
and the exudate of metal cups, that
perspiration that deadens the friendship
clink.

Then the incessant head waggling,
tribes of flies that silently say how happy they are,
but how they hope the bruise won't get passed on
yet know it must, and will, and tell the couple how
now they can try their tongues together and call the bees.
Even the ice relents, dripping chunks of its sacred trunk
to its thighs, its toes, and then to the burnt grass
below which needs the blessing most. How dry your life,
you think, to stand back on a Saturday night
and watch it all from such a narrow slot, all
these people who seem to know one another
better than you've ever known yourself or
the way the world works. BBC news suddenly blaring
through the room, from out of the void of another power
outage, urgencies about Rwanda and Tel Aviv
and Pakistan and the Indian Parliament. Your wife taken
by the heat in a dark hotel on a strange bed
before your very eyes, lying exhausted, sipping a bottle
of Banaras Limca through a straw, mouthing the vowels
for *another power surge*, while the fan above you sputters
and slurps it all up as if your life has splintered
into four flat, sporadic slats.

And then the goodbyes, more
head waggling, touching, tears
like those great farewells of Arctic explorers
who, bundled in their parkas, know they may never
again see the local ribgrass and be warm. The bamboo
shifting of poles, tugging of gates, guests
seeping out into Banaras dust, tiny gusts
tromping in at the opening like pinhole
pricks in a balloon, oppressively hot
yet somehow river-silk. Almost like introducing
new skin into your world so the wound
might stop.

But it goes on, scabbing
and rescabbing, clasped by bindis and bangles, coated
by body paint, bitten by flies, scratched
with ice, welcomed at the banks
by long pink tongues that momentarily work the crust
into strange, exotic cud. Tongues that even try
to touch hurt in places they cannot
possibly reach. Mole-flecked beneath chins, pus-filled
behind twitching ears. Blistered and exposed, even,
on the swatting tail itself. And the backs. Especially
along the backs. Magnificent bellowing necks
arching plates back into those mounds that keep trying
to bury the wrathful kisses of flies, brown slabs
that lumber through narrow lanes to the banks,
massive continents that one day give in
to their weight and slip into oceans, displacing
the flood. And the mewlings.
The pink attempt at getting the tenderness
just right, tongues that moistly dart at you rose-tinted
from the half-light swords
of a hotel fan, that narrow corridor of bleached blood
between East and West, London and Tel Aviv, Pakistan
and India, sickness and health. Young tongues
and old, bold tongues or shy, arranged
tongues or love, that try together
on their night for what always seems the first time
to lick the bites and cull the bees
and all their humming home.
Tongues that never seem to stay
long enough before returning to tunnels
of dark muzzles that float thin beards awhile
on holy Ganges waves, then seek puddles, slosh,
and mud as a way to lie down, to finally quell
the flies, cure the hides.

THE
SHAPE
OF
DISSOLVE

SUDDENLY, THE DEATH

"I die daily."
—St. Paul, cited by Paramahansa Yogananda as expressing
the inner teachings of yoga, in which the yogi learns to "die"
to the outer sensorium and the world of the ego.

Various silences slip off
into the limp of the lame about you.
Talk about *this,* action over *that.*
Stars dissolve within their primitive
impulse. India was once ruled by great kings,
and even greater yogis retreated to caves,
created the heavens without leaving
their grass mats and deerskin seats.
Mapped an inner astrology
of ascent, altar of the spine.
Constellations calm the death
of a gold carp suddenly stoked ashore.
She, where no one speaks even of bamboo
smoldering on the far bank of the Ganges.
George Seferis never practiced meditation.
Still, he knew enough of the color orange
to let each new poem "dry" like a generation
of wood for a future violin bow
as he traveled from Athens
to Kifissia and back again
to sound.

You move inside the breath
within the breath, revolve Jupiter deep
in the spine's cool and warm currents.
There is the texture of a burning
oak as you contemplate coffins of the future,
planets of possibility, precisely twelve—
six, front and back—in sacred succession.
Gold carp jack fruit mirrors,
the sadhu tells you, but only

with his leafy nonrestless breath,
that canopy of calm. She, your Divine Mother,
where no one speaks even
a seeking, even the fin-flash
of a blood orange in the long bone
of the moon lodged in your throat.
Sunrise in Seferis's Cephalonia
is moon-burn in early evening gauze
of the Ganges? Six chakras of the exact egg
are, by polarity, the twelve orbiting cracks
of our solar system?
Gold carp jack fruit mirrors.
Gold carp jack fruit mirrors.

Primitive caves retreat
back through branching
nerve ganglia into the impulse
of the spine, as if seeing
repeats itself to sound,
to vowel, to sound
dissolve. Various stars
shed their created heavens, alter
talk and *limp, action* and *slip.*
The bow maker says, No,
not he, but his son will one day make the wood
piles into bows, for *the wood has not yet dried.*
How many know to wait? asked Seferis.

Though submerged in a pool,
a gold carp smolders in gold.

SARNATH AND THE SHAPE OF DISSOLVE

for Mary Ann

1. Shards of a Bowl

Among ruins at Sarnath, you take the path
that Buddha took 2,500 years ago. You enter an indentation

of stones, an intonation of *OM*—remnants
of an altar, outline of a door, shards of a bowl—

and are surprised to discover a deer
across the field, poking a weed, stripping tufts

of bark and fur from a tree. You try to quiet
your thoughts. A sparrow flits, almost unnoticed,

like a tiny brown flare at the back of your mind.
Is it a light brown calm coming upon you

or a dithering down deep, constant beneath perception?
You are unsure of the question, unsure, even,

if a question can be cast as *either* and *or*,
if a question itself can really exist

apart from an answer. You see a monk
in prayer bowing an orange wave before a brown stupa,

two kids on the corner selling bottles of Pepsi and Limca.
An autorickshaw coughs diesel as it takes a curve.

All moments exist as a collision of instance,
or as a moment of crisis? You turn to photograph

your wife beneath a flowering bougainvillea,
are stunned by the brilliance

of each petal, by the permanence of Dhamekh Stupa
brown and massive behind her, her smile dissolving

borders of shape and color, emerging
from, blending into, a circle

of stone and diverted branch,
feather-flutter and reddening leaves.

2. The Middle Way

Left right, right left. Yes no, no yes.
A bougainvillea shifts in wind.
Ashoka, the great Buddhist emperor,
built a stone pillar, over twenty meters high,

inscribing upon it the law of The Middle Way.
You touch the remains in front of the Main Shrine.
How many souls mouthed the words, you are unsure,
but you are certain many died passing them

as law, maintaining their awe
against Muslim invaders from the north. You feel
your whole body milch a moment
with the stress, even, of a drop

to 115-degree heat, with the tourniquet
of history. Pad into the museum for relief,
see the capital of the pillar removed
for posterity. Four back-to-back lions roar

forward, blossom over an elephant,
horse, and bull. The lion
symbolizes bravery, you were told. The elephant,
the dream Buddha's mother had before he was born.

The horse, how Buddha left home on horseback
in search of enlightenment. The bull,
no one can say for sure. There is a soreness
in the attendant's voice as he scolds you

with loud Hindi, with exact hands, for asking
to take a photo. *Right left, left
right. No yes, yes no.* Outside, a bougainvillea
shifts in wind, milting red blossoms to earth.

3. The Motion of Carp

A bo tree growing in Sarnath
                    at the Mulgandha
        Kuti-Vihar
                        is a transplant from the
                            tree

            in Anuradhapura, Sri Lanka,
            which in turn
                is said
            to be an offspring
                            of the original tree

                under which the Buddha attained
        enlightenment. The mind moves
    back   the sun moves

                            onto a carved brown stupa
                        in Buddhist temple grounds.

            Does the movement back
            bring one closer

            to an original moment,

a point of light

that

dissolves

stone   sitting quietly
in your brain
like an unticking

clock? You reset your watch
to account for the India shift
in time.
      Is morning here the same
or different from morning
in the States? Do we have a way

of asking the question
and allowing for time
to exist

only
in the motion
of

a carp that
goes
gold to black, black to

gold,

in a temple pool?

You have traveled
to the other side
of the earth

and still pronounce *Casio*
with a limp of
              English

as you try to learn the Hindi word
for *hour*,
         minute,
                  second. You might bathe

         in a 4,000-year-old kund
         and still miss the carp—

         stunned by the persistence
         of green scum
         clinging to the bottom and sides—

         sensing them
                  like ghosts   at the periphery
      of a pool,
                  a box of filmy water,

      the stopped breath

      of a photograph
      when the tip of someone's finger
      or strap of camera

   slices through the border

4. What the Past Brings

Thus, the great Gautama Buddha,
having sat in the shade of a tree, having
surfaced from samadhi, having
emerged from the forest, having survived

the scorn of his fellow ascetics for claiming
The Middle Way, spoke:

    Silence is the parataxis of language

    All words are green scum; thus hold to the carp

    Wanting to not hold, a form of shoulder

    Wanting to not want: the only thing to want

    Forsake everything but everything

    Water forsakes water in the belly of a deer

    What is the sound of one deer dying?

    What is the drone of your hand on damp sheets?

    Liquid stones! Liquid stones! Liquid stones!

    All matter is conjugated energy

    Your car battery confiscates the hum of bees

    Electric blankets house hobbled lightning

    Computer screens comb folds of solidified sound

    Email is a lower form called "linear **OM**"

    Your VCR parboils paramecia

Your DVDs anesthetize amoebas

Bread caught in the toaster is burnt bread

Bread caught in the blender is out of place

What is the sound of one blender grinding?

Grain molting green is a bad photograph border

Carp scum in a tank is your insides bleeding green

Thus, the great Gautama Buddha,
having surfaced from samadhi, having
emerged from the forest, having survived the scorn
of his fellow ascetics—no, wait. Did he thus spake,

or did thus spake you? What makes a word or phrase
change or skew? Did you spake him, or
did he spake you? And when might *spake* become *speak,*
and how might a word thrust forward from *deer bellies*

to *car batteries* to *carp scum* consummate the curve
of sound you now mouth to be? And why is the rhythm
of each aphorism cast in eight to twelve English beats
(except for the secret one that contains *thirteen*)?

You bring from the past what the past brings you.
You take from the path what the path might do.
Left yes, right no. Chaos in order. Mortar in worlds
within whirls, colliding within words, words within pearls.

5. The Shape of Dissolve

You continue among the ruins, bent toward
a feeding of *OM*, waiting leopard

skin, anticipated bliss of the Buddha. Shards
of a bowl. A sparrow disturbs your quiet,

or does your quiet disturb—even augment—its flight?
A question cast as *either* and *or* is not a real

question but a Cartesian fix keeping you
from dissolve. The orange wave of a monk approaches

Dhamekh Stupa like a fiery tongue at an infinite
brown shore. It begins to rain. You understand

Takahashi Shinkichi in the press of palm leaves,
in the gaze of a young couple holding hands

near Deer Park, *The sparrow is the mightiest
creature in the world*. You approach the boys

selling Pepsi and Limca, request an Indian cola,
Thumbs Up, are comforted from the heat.

But the carbonation brings a familiar burn
to your esophagus, making you recall that in 1961

someone poured a bottle of cola on the bumper of a Buick
and rusted it out. You avoid it at home in Indiana

but require the sugar and caffeine in India
heat. Or do you need something more? The shift

and vowel of two letters more? You consider those two
remaining sounds, *n* and *a*, rolling them into a single point

of negation: *na. India-na*, you say. *India-
na*, you repeat over and again, mouthing the syllables

in the slow motion of a goldfish testing borders
of a bowl. *India-na*, you tongue once more, as if

you are saying *no* to dust, sweat, religious wars,
quiet, poverty, Pepsi, peace. As if none of these exist

back home. As if you are affirming Indiana—a place
you've never really loved—and dismissing what you know

of where you are right now. And where you are is
at Ashoka's pillar, moved by the cut of letters

charting The Middle Way, but unable to decipher
the script. And where you are is Deer Park,

watching the spark of young love where Buddha bathed
his first sermon. And where you are is a fleck of Sarnath

sun dissolving a broken bowl. And where you are
is a deep pool flickering a carp in a drop

of bleached sun. And where you are is a bougainvillea
with your wife's smile, a brilliant blossom

that will last, a monoecious fire
that will neither live nor sky, dissolve

nor sound, air nor ground,
as you carpellate the path that, barefoot,

Buddha pressed 2,500 years ago, as you begin to read
ruins for *liquid stones, liquid stones, liquid*

stones and for the splay of light as a golden thread
of carp and a shade to finally be *water*

forsaking water in the belly of a deer. As you see
the burn of a bougainvillea leaf in the motion

of your wife's eyes slowed
to underwater speech, and begin

the slow walk back to dissolve.
As you begin and begin and begin and begin.

Afterword

I came to the teachings of India in 1972, although it wasn't until 1984 that I took up a serious study and practice of the Hindu-yogic tradition. Thus, my 1994 journey to the motherland was the culmination of many years of keen anticipation. My stay in India was as profound and awful (in the sense of evoking "awe") as I had imagined, perhaps more so, and my first book, *The Theory and Function of Mangoes,* chronicled it, written in a heat shortly upon my return to the States and revised over the next several years. This current volume has gestated much longer—for better or worse—with most of the poems coming from 1996–1998, the poems and their sequencing undergoing countless revisions throughout the last decade.

I went to India not to aesthetically colonize it but, in part, to more clearly understand and engage my practice within its cultural context. India, I soon discovered, was paradoxical—surprisingly familiar to me, terrible yet wonderful, indeed "awful" in the most profound meaning of that word.

Although this book continues chronicling my months abroad, it should not be considered a sequel to *The Theory and Function of Mangoes* but an alternate, at times parallel, movement. As just one (technical) example, I wrote *Mangoes* almost entirely in enjambed couplets, as one way to foreground the need to dissolve dichotomous renderings—of East and West, self and other, even, on a physiological level, the duality that the inhalation and exhalation suggest. This current volume, while often returning to this structure as its bass tone, expands upon it, perhaps the way a gold carp itself tests the depths for the proper balance and texture of food. Those readers familiar with my poetry know that it has been my practice to work on several books concurrently over many years, my process inadvertently subverting any attempt to chronologically map "developments," "tendencies," or "trends." Brahms wrote four symphonies, though they sound like large movements of some single greater whole. Brah*man*—that energy that pervades all—continues to unfold throughout the universe without particular attachment to time, sequence, or chronology.

—George Kalamaras
Livermore, Colorado / Fort Wayne, Indiana
July 2006–September 2007

INDIAN TERMS

Terms are defined at the time of their first appearance and often appear in subsequent poems as well.

The Crawl of Ash

Banaras: a former name of Varanasi and the most sacred city in India, commonly considered throughout India as the "oldest continuously inhabited city on earth."

Jasmine

rickshaw: a small two-wheeled carriage in which passengers are transported. The old rickshaws, pulled by men, are outlawed throughout India except in Calcutta and in one or two hill stations. Most are now bicycle-powered rickshaws.

wallah: seller of certain goods or provider of services (as in rickshaw wallah).

lungi: similar to a sarong; worn by men, especially of the lower castes.

rupee: the main form of currency in India; in 1994, one rupee equaled approximately three United States cents.

Sacrifice

Ganga: the Ganges River.

sitar: a stringed instrument of India, made of seasoned gourds and teak, containing either six or seven playing strings and thirteen sympathetic resonating strings.

Brahma: a Hindu deity, the Creator.

The Milk of Shadows

Durga: a Hindu deity and form of the Divine Mother in one of Her benevolent aspects.

ji: a suffix often added to names as a sign of endearment and respect (for instance, Gandhiji, Babaji, etc.).

chai: Indian tea, made with sugar and milk.

sadhu: Hindu holy man.

Banaras is Another Name for the World
dal: cooked soupy lentil dish.

ghat: steep steps leading down to a river, where pilgrims perform ritual bathing (bathing ghat) or are cremated (cremation ghat). Banaras is well known for its long string of bathing and cremation ghats that line the west bank of the Ganges River.

In Bhelupur
Limca: citrus-flavored, light-colored soft drink.

Handling Fruit at a Calcutta Market
Calcutta: the former name of Kolkata. Since it, and Mumbai's previous name, Bombay, had not changed by the time of my stay in India, I have relied upon their earlier names throughout, which were used widely while I was there. In part to standardize, I have also used the former names of Banaras and Poona for Varanasi and Pune, respectively.

Baba: father; a term of respect for men; also a term often given to male sadhus.

What is Open
harmonium: an organ-like keyboard, common in India, that produces tones with free metal reeds actuated by air forced from a bellows.

sweeper: lowest category in the Hindu caste system; a fifth group below the four castes, often referred to as "untouchable"; a member of this group who performs menial labor.

You Keep Coming Upon Your Breath at the Altar
Ananda Moyi Ma: highly adept woman saint (yogini) of the twentieth century.

diksha: initiation into spiritual practices.

baksheesh: tip; a request for money often used by beggars.

The Lamps Are Brought In

Kali: a Hindu deity representing, on a symbolic level, the Void from which the potential, creative force springs. Kali is the "dark" or "black" goddess. Although by some accounts in Hindu literature, Kali represents all three aspects of divine experience—the creative, preservative, and destructive— she is predominantly associated with the "destructive" or "dissolving" force (or Void) that dissolves back into itself all physical manifestations (the creative activity of Shiva) that have issued from it. Kali, as a destructive force or Void, is not considered "evil" (in the Western sense) in Hindu scriptures but contains the creative *potential* of the Void, acting as a complement to Shiva. Thus, although dark and dissolving, Kali simultaneously represents the At-one-ment that is regarded as light and bliss.

Tantric: of or relating to Tantra, a form of Yoga of obscure origin, which emphasizes the awakening of Kundalini (see note under "At the Ashram of Trailanga Swami"), the all-powerful sacred energy that lies dormant at the base of the spine.

puja: prayer or worship.

pakora: vegetable fritter made with sweet chickpea flour batter, and a traditional Indian street food.

Shiva: a Hindu deity representing, on the symbolic level, the "masculine" principle of the universe. Shiva is one of the most important gods of Hindu worship, most often depicted as an ascetic yogi of great self-control. He is occasionally depicted as the husband of Kali, the terrible goddess; when Kali's foot steps on the chest of Shiva's prostrate body, the "creative" activity of the universe dissolves into the Void. Hindu mythology also describes Lord Shiva as "catching" the Ganges River in his hair, cushioning its fall centuries ago as it descended from the heavens to earth. Banaras is considered "the city of Shiva."

rishi: holy person; seer. The rishis were, in antiquity, the authors of the *Vedas.*

Dhobi Wallah
dhobi: one who washes clothes, usually by hand.

pan: betel nut plus chewing additives and various pastes, wrapped in a damp green leaf, and sold in street stalls as a mild stimulant; the chewing of pan often emits a red juice that stains the teeth and corners of the mouth.

kurta: a shirt, normally blouse-like, with a long square tail to the knees.

pajama: pants tied at the waist with a drawstring.

Convergence
vegetable korma: spicy vegetable dish.

Nahin: Hindi for "no."

Landscape of the Dead
sari: a length of lightweight cloth worn as a garment by women.

Lodi Gardens: beautiful gardens in Delhi, containing magnificent Mogul tombs of the Sayyid and Lodi rulers.

doams: a traditional community of outcasts (chandal) who manage the cremation ghats.

A Theory of the Function of the Confusion of Things
pronam: a greeting in which both hands are joined at the palms, in front of a person's chest or forehead, as a sign of respect.

mantra: a word or phrase with a particular sound and/or verbal significance. Various mantras, carrying differing psychological and physical effects, are often used in Hindu meditative practices for communing with or attaining to the divine (or unified) experience. They are said to evoke particular states of consciousness and/or material effects.

rudraksha beads: strings of Hindu holy beads made from the dried pits of fruit and either worn around the neck or held in the hands to help count the repetitions of mantras or to mark other sacred rituals; ancient rishis (Indian seers) and modern yogis claim that when worn against the skin, rudraksha beads emit helpful electric currents to the body, conducive for good health and deeper meditation.

dhoti: garment; a loincloth worn by men.

Karmic Seeds
Nilakantha: a form of the Hindu deity Shiva. Nilakantha has a blue throat, a result of swallowing the poison that otherwise would have destroyed the world.

padyatra: excursion (by foot) of politicians to seek support at the village level.

Next Year When I Fish Hydrates in Fiscal Blue
Poona: a former name of Pune, a city in the Indian state of Maharashtra.

Krishna: one of the most important of the Hindu deities and hero of one of the greatest Hindu scriptures, the *Bhagavad-Gita*. Krishna—most often colored blue—is the eighth incarnation of another important deity, Vishnu.

Scales of Mother Ganga
Aghori: sect, or religious order, of Hindu sadhus, whose practices are rooted in Tantra.

The Cobra: yogic asana (posture).

ek-bahu Baba: "one-arm" Baba (father); an ascetic who practices the austerity of keeping one arm continuously raised for a specified number of years.

A Temple Pool Might Ignite (Lotus-Blood from Your Heart)
lassi: a sweet yogurt and iced-water drink common in India.

Bhagavad-Gita: one of the most sacred Indian scriptures.

Gold Carp Jack Fruit Mirrors
stupa: a Buddhist monument or shrine.

Kashi: the scriptural name of the holy city of Banaras.

samadhi: ecstatic state of mystical union with the divine, most often a result of deep yogic meditation.

Shiva's wild, matted hair: see note near the end of Shiva, "The Lamps Are Brought In."

Sarnath: a major Buddhist center, just ten kilometers from Banaras, and site of Buddha's first sermon after he achieved enlightenment. Later, Ashoka, a significant Buddhist emperor, erected stupas and "Ashoka's Pillar" here.

Parvati: a Hindu deity and form of the Divine Mother in one of Her benevolent aspects.

At Red Fort
mulligatawny: a lentil soup.

At the Taj Mahal
kund: pond, usually containing sacred waters. Krim Kund is an ancient sacred pond at the site of the Aghori ashram in Banaras.

Icon
thali: Indian meal of assorted curry vegetable dishes, breads, rice, and sometimes dessert, normally served on a single platter.

Lolark Kund: a deep pond in Banaras, normally sixty feet deep during monsoon, surrounded by cemented walls of sandstone. Water flows from the kund into a well, and then into the Ganges. The god Lolark is worshipped here, as the Sun, at this ancient site of what is believed to be auspicious, healing waters.

Cut of the World
Thumbs Up and Gold Spot: two flavors of Indian soft drinks.

lichi: a small juicy fruit, with a reddish tough skin.

At the Ashram of Trailanga Swami
Trailanga Swami: highly adept yogi of Banaras, believed to have weighed more than 300 pounds and to have lived nearly 300 years.

Kundalini: the all-powerful cosmic energy that, according to yogic teachings, is said to lie dormant at the base of the spine. As such, it is often symbolically depicted as a coiled serpent. In kundalini yoga—an advanced technique that, as yogic and Tantric texts advise, should be undertaken only with the guidance of a realized teacher—the yogi attempts to arouse this all-powerful potential psychic energy in a variety of ways. Upon awakening of the Kundalini energy, the yogi is said to attain cosmic consciousness and, thus, freedom from the duality of the multiplicity of conceptual awareness and the constraints of subject/object duality.

lingam: phallic symbol, representing Shiva, worshipped in many parts of India.

Getting the Tonguing Tender Enough
Ganesh (or Ganesha): a Hindu deity, with an elephant head and the body of a boy, who is depicted as riding a rat. He is the son of Parvati and Shiva.

bindi: circular colored dot worn on the forehead by married women.

Sarnath and the Shape of Dissolve
Deer Park: another name for Sarnath, site of the Buddha's first sermon. See note under *Sarnath* in "Gold Carp Jack Fruit Mirrors." Also a specific wooded area in Sarnath.

NOTES

What is Open

The phrase, "Avoid Calcutta's unhealthy monsoon / from June until the end of September," is from a guidebook, *India: A Travel Survival Kit*. Crowther, Geoff, et al. Fourth Edition. Berkeley: Lonely Planet Publications, 1990.

You Keep Coming Upon Your Breath at the Altar

The phrase attributed to Takahashi Shinkichi (in this and in "Sarnath and the Shape of Dissolve")—"The sparrow is the mightiest creature in the world"—is an adaptation from his writings in *Triumph of the Sparrow: Zen Poems of Shinkichi Takahashi*. Translated by Lucien Stryk (with the assistance of Takashi Ikemoto). Champaign: University of Illinois Press, 1986.

Convergence

The list of ailments ("rheumatism, / convulsions, scabies, boils, dysentery, ulcers, // typhoid, malaria, even prolapse of the anus") and the quote ("six lovemakings a night / to give birth to four sons") are from Pallava Bagla's "Predator." In *Travelers' Tales: India*. O'Reilly, James and Larry Habegger, eds. San Francisco: Travelers' Tales, Inc., 1995.

A Theory of the Function of the Confusion of Things

This poem was inspired by the premise of Arthur Sze's poem, "Mistaking Water Hemlock for Parsley," from his book, *River River*. Providence, RI: Lost Roads Press, 1987.

At the Taj Mahal

The phrase, "Whoever would bathe in this water / for five Tuesdays and Sundays would also be free // from his suffering," is a slightly edited version of a quote from a little booklet (from the Aghori ashram in Banaras) about the life of Baba Kina Ram. (Publication information in Hindi.) I acknowledge this—as well as the sadhus who told me other stories about Baba Kina Ram and Krim Kund—with deepest gratitude.

Suddenly, the Death

The phrase, "the wood has not yet dried. / How many know to wait?" is a paraphrase from a story told by George Seferis. *A Poet's Journal: Days of 1945-1951*. Translated by Athan Anagnostopoulos. Cambridge: Belknap Press of Harvard University, 1974.

Epigraphs are taken from the following texts:

Vedanta Press, *The Upanishads: Breath of the Eternal*. Translated by Swami Prabhavananda and Frederick Manchester. Copyright © 1948 by the Vedanta Society of Southern California. Hollywood, California.

Beacon Press, *The Poetics of Space*. Gaston Bachelard. Translated by Maria Jolas. Copyright © 1958 by Presses Universitaires de France. Translation copyright © 1964 by the Orion Press. First Beacon paperback, 1969. Used by permission of Viking Penguin, a division of Penguin Books USA, Inc.

Yoshioka Minoru. *Lilac Garden: Poems of Minoru Yoshioka*. Translated by Hiroaki Sato. Chicago: Chicago Review Press, 1976.

Paramahansa Yogananda, *Autobiography of a Yogi*. Los Angeles: Self-Realization Fellowship, 1998.

About the Author

George Kalamaras is Professor of English at Indiana University-Purdue University Fort Wayne, where he has taught since 1990. He is the author of five previous books of poetry, three of which are full-length, *Even the Java Sparrows Call Your Hair* (Quale Press, 2004), *Borders My Bent Toward* (Pavement Saw Press, 2003), and *The Theory and Function of Mangoes* (Four Way Books, 2000), which won the Four Way Books Intro Series, chosen by Michael Burkard. His poems have appeared in numerous journals and anthologies in the United States, Canada, Greece, India, Japan, Mexico, Thailand, the United Kingdom, and elsewhere, including *The Best American Poetry 2008* and *1997, The Bitter Oleander, Epoch, Hambone, New American Writing, New Letters, Sulfur, Talisman, TriQuarterly*, and others. He is the recipient of Creative Writing Fellowships from the National Endowment for the Arts (1993) and the Indiana Arts Commission (2001), and first prize in the 1998 *Abiko Quarterly* International Poetry Prize (Japan). A long-time practitioner of yogic meditation, he is also the author of a 1994 scholarly book on Hindu mysticism and Western language theory from State University of New York Press, *Reclaiming the Tacit Dimension: Symbolic Form in the Rhetoric of Silence*. During 1994, he spent several months in India on an Indo-U.S. Advanced Research Fellowship from the Fulbright Foundation and the Indo-U.S. Subcommission on Education and Culture. He lives in Fort Wayne, Indiana with his wife, the writer Mary Ann Cain, and their beagle, Barney, and they often return to northern Colorado, where George and Mary Ann lived for several years in the 1980s.